KU-650-974

# Divorce and Remarriage in the Church

Biblical solutions for pastoral realities

# Divorce and Remarriage in the Church

## Biblical solutions for pastoral realities

David Instone-Brewer

**Paternoster:**
*thinking faith*

Copyright © 2003 David Instone-Brewer

First published in 2003 by Paternoster
Reprinted 2004, 2006, 2011

17 16 15 14 13 12 11   10 9 8 7 6 5 4

Reprinted 2011 by Paternoster
Paternoster is an imprint of Authentic Media Limited
Presley Way, Crownhill, Milton Keynes, MK8 0ES
www.authenticmedia.co.uk

The right of David Instone-Brewer to be
identified as the Author of this Work has been
asserted by him in accordance with
Copyright, Designs and Patents Act 1988

All rights reserved. No part of this publication may be reproduced, stored
in a retrieval system, or transmitted in any form or by any means,
electronic, mechanical, photocopying, recording or otherwise, without the
prior permission of the publisher or a licence permitting restricted copying.
In the UK such licences are issued by the Copyright Licensing Agency,
Saffron House, 6-10 Kirby Street, London, EC1N 8TS

**British Library Cataloguing in Publication Data**

A catalogue record for this book is available from
the British Library

ISBN 978-1-84227-180-3

Biblical quotations are from the English Standard Version Crossway Bible,
2001, except where indicated.

Cover design by Paul Airy at DesignLeft (www.designleft.co.uk)
Printed and Bound in Great Britain by Bell and Bain, Glasgow

# Contents

# Preface

This book has been through several incarnations and has benefited from the input of many people, especially the congregation of Llanishen Baptist Church and my fellow minister Michael Ball, who all suffered several sermons on this subject while I was working through these ideas. My wife, Enid, has been equally long-suffering and has frequently steered me from theory to practical issues.

Most of the academic work which forms the foundation of this book has been published as papers in various scholarly journals and in my academic book on this topic, *Divorce and Remarriage in the Bible – the social and literary context* (Eerdmans, 2002). This work was largely done as a Research Fellow at Tyndale House in Cambridge, and I do not think that it would have been possible to investigate fully all the varied aspects of the cultural background to the Biblical text without the unequalled resources of their superb library.

The readability of this book is due solely to Sheron Rice who edited the book so diligently that she virtually rewrote the whole work and still managed to use most of my words. This book would not exist without her.

My aim in writing this book is to share insights which enabled me to understand the issue of divorce and remarriage through the eyes of the first readers of the New Testament. My hope is that the church will rediscover the Biblical principles that divorce should only occur when marriage vows are broken, and that only the wronged partner may decide whether this will happen. When people see that the church has practical and straightforward guidance to give on this subject, they may listen to its message that marriage should be life-long and that no-one should divorce unless there are serious grounds for it.

# Introduction

## What's new?

"So, what do you do for a living?" the young man asked me with a barely stifled yawn. He was trying to sell me a time-share apartment and I was trying to get a free holiday without buying anything. I had to pretend to be interested in his product and he had to pretend to be interested in me.

"I study the Bible at a research institute in Cambridge."

He looked up suspiciously, as though he had caught me lying: "I thought they'd have finished studying the Bible by now. What else is left for you to find out?"

I'd like to say that I took the opportunity to present the Gospel to him, but I think I merely assured him that this was indeed what I did for a living and that there was lots of Biblical research left to be done.

It's an unfortunate fact that there are still significant gaps in our knowledge of the language, culture and archaeology of the Bible. The 1st century especially has been less well understood because fewer non-Biblical documents have survived than from surrounding centuries. At present, however, our knowledge of the 1st century is expanding rapidly because we are beginning to understand properly the Dead Sea Scrolls and early Rabbinic traditions as well as new scraps of ancient texts which are still being published.

The findings in this book are based on a multitude of new discoveries and academic publications by myself and others. The most important of these are as follows:

- Dead Sea Scroll fragments dealing with divorce, which help us to understand the other scrolls.

- Newly discovered Jewish divorce certificates such as one written by a Jewish man in Masada in AD 72 and one written by a Jewish woman in about AD 125.

- Over 200 Aramaic, Greek and Latin marriage and divorce papyri which have been collected together for the first time.

- Rabbinic evidence which can now be dated to the 1st century.

- Publication of hundreds of new Samaritan documents, including ancient marriage contracts.

- Publication and analysis of all the Rabbinic and Karaite marriage and divorce documents from the Geniza of the Cairo Synagogue.

This wealth of new information gives us a much greater understanding of how people spoke and lived in the 1st century and, as a result, we can read the New Testament with fresh insight. We are closer than ever before to understanding what it meant to its very first hearers and readers – and to understanding what God says to us today.

# 1

# Confessions of a Confused Minister

**Jesus never said: "What God has joined, no man can separate"**

I was being interviewed for what would be my first church pastorate and I was nervous and unsure what to expect. The twelve deacons sat in a row in front of me and took turns to ask questions which I answered as clearly as I could. All went reasonably smoothly and then came the really tricky one: "What is your position on divorce and remarriage? Would you remarry a divorcee?"

I didn't know if this was a trick question or simply an honest one. There might have been a deep-seated pastoral need behind it or it might have been a test of my orthodoxy. Either way, I didn't think I could summarise my view in one sentence and, when I thought about it further, I couldn't decide what exactly my view was. I gave a deliberately vague reply: "Well, I guess it depends. Every case should be judged on its own merits."

It sounded good to me – and fortunately it must have sounded good to them, because they offered me the job – but I made a mental note to put a bit of study into the subject of divorce, quickly.

## So many questions

It's a good thing I made that decision because I soon needed a real answer to what had until then been merely a hypothetical question. My Baptist church was in a suburb with an Anglican and two Catholic churches nearby. Divorcees from these churches came to us asking if we would conduct their new wedding. The Anglicans would say something along these lines: "Our vicar says we can't remarry in our church. He told us to get remarried in the Registry Office and, after that, we could have a church blessing, but we want to say our vows before God, not to a civil Registrar."

The Catholics had an additional problem: "My priest advised me to get my previous marriage annulled, but that would mean that it wasn't legally valid." I remember one particularly upset man saying, "I don't want to make my children into bastards", and although Catholic theologians would say that isn't quite the way it works, it is how many people regard an annulment. All this made me very concerned that I found the right response to give to these sincere Christians.

Then I found that some of my deacons were remarried divorcees. Should I throw them out of church leadership? If I did, I realised I'd be losing people I believed to be some of the most spiritual in the church, who had exemplary Christian homes and marriages which God appeared to have blessed.

I was surrounded by people who needed the right answer – but what was the right answer? I had always found the Bible passages about this to be confusing and contradictory.

- Why did Jesus sometimes say no to divorce and sometimes allow it?

- Why did Jesus allow divorce only for adultery while Paul allowed it only for desertion?

- Why was remarriage equivalent to adultery, even though it was after a divorce for adultery?

So I hit the books. Well, more specifically, one book – the Bible – and I was surprised by what I read. I wasn't surprised by the content because I had read all the relevant passages many times before, but I was surprised because this time it suddenly made sense.

It had been some time since I'd last looked at these passages properly and in the meantime I'd done a PhD in 1st-century Rabbinic Judaism. Whilst doing this I think I'd read everything the early Jews had written so that this time, when I read the familiar New Testament texts again, I was now doing so through the eyes of a 1st-century Jew – the people to whom Jesus and Paul had addressed their teaching. All these difficult texts on divorce and remarriage became clear.

Maybe not quite *all* the texts. I still had some questions to answer and some work to do. I didn't really understand the ancient Near

Eastern context of Moses when he wrote down the ancient laws of the Jews given to him by God at Mount Sinai and I didn't understand all the Greek legal jargon in Paul's writings. I had to go and check up a lot of Jewish  documents again, but broadly speaking the problems and contradictions which I had been used to seeing before now became perfectly clear – and what's more, their teaching was sensible.

The trouble with most theologies of divorce is that they *aren't* sensible. They may give a reasonable account for most of the texts, in a forced kind of way, but their conclusions just aren't practical in the fallen world we inhabit.

Most of society feels that the Bible has nothing sensible to say about divorce and remarriage, and even many Christians feel that they can ignore the Scriptures on this particular subject. The laws of Western nations, which are based largely on Biblical principles, have deliberately decided to avoid the issue of grounds for divorce by allowing no-fault divorce. This has resulted in a huge increase in divorces as well as a feeling that marriage can be ended by just about anything, and this in turn has resulted in disillusionment with the whole institution of marriage.

## Traditional church teaching

People have interpreted what the Bible says about divorce and remarriage in two main ways (although there are many others):

1. There are two valid grounds for divorce, but remarriage is not allowed unless one of the couple has died.
2. There are no grounds for divorce or even for separation.

The first interpretation is the one given by most established churches. They conclude that Jesus and Paul both taught that there was one valid ground for divorce (although these were different). Jesus allowed the divorce of someone who had an adulterous partner and Paul allowed the divorce of someone whose non-believing partner had deserted them. It goes on to say that neither Jesus nor Paul allowed remarriage unless one of the couple had died because, in some sense, a marriage is still valid until it is ended by death. The main problem with this interpretation is that it is illogical: why do Jesus and Paul identify these two grounds for divorce, but not allow divorce for physical abuse or other harmful situations?

The second main interpretation – which doesn't allow divorce for any reason – is more logical. It says that Jesus' ground for adultery only applied to ancient Jews because, according to their laws, adultery led to compulsory divorce. It then says that Paul's ground for desertion by a non-Christian partner was, similarly, just for ancient Romans, because under Roman law desertion was equivalent to compulsory divorce. This interpretation tells modern believers that divorce is not allowed unless you are divorced against your will and that remarriage is not allowed unless you are widowed. Although this interpretation is more logical than the first, it is even less practical because it means that someone can continue to commit adultery or physical abuse in the knowledge that their partner cannot end the marriage.

Other believers have decided that the Bible just isn't practical about these matters, so they have formulated their own "sensible" conclusion and tried to justify it according to Scripture. They say, for example, that divorce is allowed for adultery, abuse and abandonment committed by both non-believing and believing partners, and base this teaching on the principles which they extrapolate from the text by sometimes dubious means. This type of interpretation comes out of a pastoral heart and a desire to help those who are in such awful situations, and whilst I commend and agree wholeheartedly with that desire, I believe that it is far safer to arrive at a solution by looking at Scripture first and then following where it leads.

## No blinding flash

Suddenly realising how a 1st-century Jew would have understood these texts wasn't due to a blinding flash of inspiration, but was the result of three years of hard work for my PhD which suddenly came together: three years of reading huge sections of Rabbinic literature, digging into the Mishnah, Tosephta Talmud, Midrashim, Philo and the Dead Sea Scrolls; analysing the texts – especially to see how they interpreted the Old Testament – and comparing my findings with medieval and modern scholars. At the end of all this I could think and interpret like the ancient Rabbis themselves and I was able to unpack the highly abbreviated accounts of their debates.

When I re-read the words of Jesus and Paul, I found details which would have been recognised by a contemporary Rabbi, but which are meaningless to most modern readers. Both Jesus and Paul used the language and terminology used by the Rabbis – especially when speaking about divorce, which was a hot topic of debate at that time.

I suppose it's not surprising that they did so because Jesus was, after all, answering questions which were being posed by Pharisaic Rabbis, and Paul said that he had been trained under Gamaliel, who was a foremost Rabbi of the time.

I suppose you think I'm now going to tell you what I discovered. Well, sorry, I'm not – just yet. It will take some time to explain and, until I've done so, the conclusions will have to wait. I will set it out in sections:

1. The Old Testament and God's divorce. Yes, God himself is a divorcee and I was surprised to discover how strongly the Old Testament emphasised this (chapters 2–4).
2. Jesus' and Paul's teaching on divorce and remarriage (chapters 5–7).
3. How this teaching should work and a look at marriage vows (chapters 8–10).
4. Church policy on divorce and remarriage, what churches should do now, and some emails about real-life problems (chapters 11–15).

## "No-one can separate"?

But what I will tell you now is what I *didn't* find in the Bible. Just as Captain Kirk never said, "Beam me up, Scotty," and James Cagney never said, "You dirty rat," and Sherlock Holmes never said, "Elementary, my dear Watson," the Bible never says, "Those whom God has joined, no man can separate."

It's true that Jesus did say something very similar in Matthew 19.6, but his actual words (in a few representative translations) were:

"What therefore God has joined together, let not man separate." (English Standard Version)

"What therefore God hath joined together, let not man put asunder." (King James Version)

"Therefore what God has joined together, let man not separate." (New International Version)

"No human being must separate, then, what God has joined together." (Good News Bible)

None of these translations of Jesus' words read "...no-one *can* separate".

Although the phrase "no-one can separate" does not sound very different from "let him not separate" or "he must not separate", there is a world of difference in meaning.

If Jesus had said, "No-one *can* separate", it would mean that divorce is impossible, since once a couple have married, they will *always* be married in God's eyes. In other words, if God has joined a couple in marriage no-one can "unjoin" them. This is an interesting idea and although there are other hints in Scripture which may seem to back it up, we will see in chapter 7 that they do not stand up to scrutiny. It is, in any case, something of a digression because as I've said, the words "no-one *can* separate" are not in Scripture.

The words that Jesus *did* say – "*let* no-one separate" – do not mean, "It's not possible for you to separate"; they mean, "It *is* possible to separate, but you should not."

To examine these words even further, when Jesus said "let him not separate" he was, in technical terms, using the imperative mood. Other possible meanings of the imperative are "should not" or "must not". Sometimes it can have a very strong sense of being an order – "Don't!" – and at other times it can indicate a much weaker tone – "Please, don't do it!" But one thing the use of the imperative can *never* mean is, "You cannot" – i.e. the phrase can't be translated, "it is impossible for you to separate" or "you are not able to separate" or "you cannot separate". What it actually means, therefore, is that separation is certainly possible, but it is wrong or, at the very least, undesirable.

So what did Jesus mean when he told people not to separate? Clearly he was saying that it is wrong, but was he talking about divorce or about separation? The Greek word he used for "separate" – *chorizo* – was the word usually used to mean "divorce" (in fact, the standard lexicon for non-literary Greek, Moulton & Milligan, even says that *chorizo* was *the* technical term for "divorce" – and although this is probably an exaggeration, it was certainly *one* of the technical terms for divorce). It's therefore clear that Jesus was making a plea or a command against *divorce* rather than separation. He wasn't saying that divorce *could not* happen but that it *shouldn't* happen.

And to whom is he saying this? Who is the sinner in a divorce? Is it the person who decides to separate and who starts the legal proceedings? Or is it the person who causes the divorce?

## Looking forward

We will see in later chapters that what defines a broken marriage is broken vows: the vows that marriage partners make to each other in God's presence. We will find in chapter 3 that the Old Testament described God's relationship with Israel like a marriage which ended in divorce because of Israel's adulteries. So God is a divorcee – and he 'hates' it as much as any victim of divorce.

A victim? Yes, God is a victim of divorce, even though he actually carried it out, and many victims today are actually the ones who initiate the proceedings to bring the marriage to an official end. They call in the lawyers to stop the mockery and pain of constant adultery, or the anguish of abuse, but as we will see, the Bible does not regard the victim as the sinner. It is the person who is guilty of causing the marriage to break up whom Jesus addressed when he said: "Those whom God has joined, no-one should separate."

In other words, his warning is not to the person who finally tidies up the legal mess after the marriage has broken down, but to those who would violate their marriage vows and, in so doing, cause the marriage to break up.

Jesus said that divorce should never happen because when a couple marry they are joined by God who is a witness to the marriage vows and is there to bless them. These vows should never be broken – especially vows made before God – but, of course, people do break them (just as they break others of God's commands). Jesus never said that these vows are impossible to break – as if God ignores the reality of sin – but he taught that if a partner breaks their vows and is then repentant, we should forgive them. If the vows are continuously broken, without repentance, then the marriage will be left in shreds. Therefore, although the break-up of a marriage is always due to sin, it is not the divorce itself that is the sin – the sin is the breaking of the vows which causes the divorce.

In later chapters we will look at the Biblical marriage vows closely. We will also learn that the Bible allows only the victim to initiate a divorce – that is, it allows them to decide when enough is enough and, if their partner remains unrepentant, to decide that the marriage is over. Jesus' main complaint was that the Jews had abandoned this principle. They allowed a man to divorce his wife even when she hadn't broken her vows, i.e. when he had no grounds for divorce. Paul similarly condemned a Graeco-Roman groundless divorce.

Later on in the book we will look at the Old Testament's teaching on divorce and remarriage – which allowed divorce on the grounds of neglect or abuse – and discover that Jesus and Paul both affirmed this teaching.

## Putting it in context

As this is all very different from what the church has been teaching for many, many years it does, I agree, make my conclusions rather suspect. There is a good reason, however, why the church has misunderstood this teaching: our knowledge of 1st-century AD language and culture was lost and critical facts about Jewish divorce had gone missing by the 2nd century.

As all good preachers know, "a text without a context is a pretext" and this is a very important truth for understanding the divorce issue. We need to know the cultural context of our texts in order to understand them. For example, we now know the reason why Paul insisted that women covered their heads in church. At that time it was highly immodest for women to go bare-headed outside their own homes and only prostitutes did so. It was also a society where morals were under constant threat, which was especially difficult for the newly emerging church. Our modern-day church, for the most part, doesn't demand that women wear hats to church although, of course, it's understandable that some people still want to keep to this teaching.

I will examine the cultural context in greater detail in later chapters and explain how we can discover what Jesus really taught about divorce. The implications of his teaching will be far more severe than the wearing of hats in church, however, and understandably many people will be reluctant to accept it.

What we have found out already is very important. We have discovered that the Bible may not say what we thought it did. Sometimes we come to the Bible already very sure about what it means and this can blind us to reading it with the Spirit's guidance. Sometimes it's necessary for us to let ourselves forget what we think we know and read it afresh. That's what I had the chance to do as a young minister and I had some extra help – an insight into how the Rabbis thought.

God has given us Scripture, which is a book of personal experiences. It is full of histories, letters, prophetic messages and praise songs. It contains almost no theology, so we are left to work out the principles for ourselves – and we won't always come to the same answers. We are gradually leaving behind misunderstandings like the inherent sinfulness of sexual contact or the belief that there is no forgiveness for sins after baptism (both of which almost all the early Church Fathers believed). And we no longer burn heretics – which is fortunate for me because some of you will conclude that I am one!

## Draw your own conclusions

My only aim in studying this topic and in writing this book has been to listen to God as he speaks to us through the Bible, and I hope that you are prepared to read the Bible again with me as I explain further. But please don't just accept what I say as being the correct interpretation. I'm not claiming any revelation from God and many Christians interpret the texts in other ways. Paul says in 1 Corinthians 14.29 that we should judge the prophets and if we are asked to judge those who bring direct revelations, then we should certainly also judge our Bible teachers. My prayer for readers of this book is that we will use Scripture, the help of the Holy Spirit, and our intelligence to judge where the truth lies and then live by our consciences.

## Further Reading

### Traditional church teaching on divorce

*Divorce and Remarriage in the Bible*, Chapter 9 "History of Divorce" by David Instone-Brewer (Eerdmans, 2002) covers the Church Fathers, the Reformers and the positions of various modern churches.

*Marriage and Divorce in the Bible and the Church* by Alex R. G. Deasley (Beacon Hill, 2000) offers an excellent review of the Church Fathers.

*Jesus and Divorce* by William A. Heth, & Gordon J. Wenham (Hodder & Stoughton, 1984), Chapters 1 and 2 – a good survey, but it tends to ignore dissent among the Church Fathers.

### Modern 'solutions' to NT divorce teaching

*Divorce & Remarriage in the Bible*, Chapter 10 "Modern Re- interpretations" summarises the huge variety of modern re-interpretations of the Bible texts.

*To Have and To Hold: The Marriage Covenant and the Discipline of Divorce* by David Atkinson (Collins, 1979) argues that abuse and neglect break the 7th commandment.

*Marriage, Divorce & Remarriage in the Bible* by Jay E. Adams, (Presbyterian and Reformed Publishing Co, 1980) argues that abuse and neglect are un-Christian, so a believer can be divorced by them.

*Putting Asunder: Divorce and Remarriage in Biblical and Pastoral Perspective* by Stephen Clark (Brynterion Press, 1999) argues that abuse and neglect show that the person is an unbeliever and does not want to remain married, so the believer can divorce them.

# 2

# A Marriage Made in Paradise

## Moses' certificate of divorce

Have you heard the one about Adam and his "spare" rib? Well, as you know, in the beginning God made Adam and put him in Paradise. Adam was allowed to enjoy all the many wonders of the Garden of Eden and was given the job of naming all the animals. But after he had named them – rather a long task – he got bored. He wanted some company. Someone he could talk to and impress. God understood the situation perfectly. "I can see that you're lonely," he said to Adam. "Let me make a woman for you."

"What's a woman?" asked Adam.

"A woman will love and adore you. She'll cook perfect meals and always look nice. She'll laugh at all your jokes and she'll never complain."

"That's wonderful!" said Adam with enthusiasm. "But... she sounds very expensive. What will she cost me?"

"Ah," replied God. "A woman like that will cost you an arm and a leg."

Adam considered this carefully for a moment, then turned back to his Maker. "What will I get for one rib?"

## God's perfect plan

OK, so men aren't perfect either – and we certainly don't live in Paradise any more. Are we asking the impossible of marriage? Can we really live happily with each other's imperfections and strange, annoying habits – let alone our tendency for downright selfishness? Even if we start off feeling that our partner can do no wrong, doesn't that phrase "the honeymoon period" sum up the truth that the blissful period of perfect love and contentment is but a short stage quickly passed through? The truth is that marriage is hard work – and many are often far from successful.

Marriages started to fail with Adam and Eve. When they were thrown out of Paradise because of their disobedience, they soon encountered difficulties, but their reduced circumstances were the least of their problems because they themselves had changed – and changed for the worse. They had both discovered the difference between good and evil, and at the heart of this discovery was the desire to do what they wanted. This wasn't necessarily what God or the other person wanted and it immediately led to conflict.

Like many couples, they also found that having children didn't bring them closer together. It's hard enough for two people to want the same thing at the same time, but when there are three or four people in the family it becomes more and more difficult for them all to agree – especially when the children start growing into independent adults. Family gatherings, such as mealtimes, often become battle grounds.

One, admittedly tongue-in-cheek, definition of the family is that it is a group of individuals who are united by a common TV set. And as a family increases and starts to fragment, the number of TVs it owns also increases. To take the analogy back to early times, a family could be identified as a group which sat around the same camp fire and when members of the same family started to sit around different fires, relationships had clearly gone seriously wrong. It wasn't long before Adam's camp had a whole constellation of fires!

God is realistic about the problems of individuals living together and from the beginning he had a plan designed to help couples stay together and which goes some way to dealing with our quarrelsome individualism.

> Gen. 2.24: Therefore a man shall leave his father and his mother and hold fast to his wife, and they shall become one flesh.

In other words, God says, "When a couple get married they must leave their parents' home and set up a new home of their own." This sounds like very simple advice, but it *is* effective and in fact was quite counter-cultural to the people of the Old Testament. Two adults will have more than enough trouble living together happily without twenty-four hours a day of 'helpful comments' from their parents.

There's a second part to God's instructions and the first part only works if we follow this as well: "When you get married, whatever happens, stick together as though you were one person."

If the advice is followed, a man and woman will get married and commit to each other totally. They will promise to stay together and try to act like one person. God tells them to leave both their family homes and make a new home – and he makes sure that no-one else joins them for at least nine months. When the new person does arrive, he or she will only gradually develop an independent will, so that the couple has time to get used to the idea of having another individual living alongside them, with their differing needs and expectations.

Children soon become individuals, of course. They quickly find out how to say "No!" when they don't want to do something. They learn how to argue and then as teenagers they begin to think seriously and may reject a lot of what their parents tell them. It's not too long before they start to notice the opposite sex and then before the parents know it, their offspring have found someone they want to marry. After a painfully expensive, though joyous, wedding, things get better. The newly-marrieds leave mum and dad to set up home together and the conflicts and frustrations experienced between parent and child are resolved. They find that their parents can be friends and confidantes rather than oppressive tyrants, and God's wisdom is proved once more.

## But in practice ...

Well – that's the theory, but more often than not it seems that marriages go wrong. Children stay at home longer now, mainly because education takes longer. Couples don't always begin with having a home just to themselves for even nine months. And they don't always learn how to accommodate each other, let alone their children. They end up battling with each other and their children rather than communicating and negotiating. Sadly, but all too commonly, people stop trying to resolve their differences and give up on their relationships instead. Children run away or, more often, one of the parents walks out. Often one parent has left long before the teenage battles with their children start, because they couldn't learn to live with their partner.

## The cruel world of the ancient Near East

The state of marriage today is certainly not healthy, but we would be wrong to assume that it is just a modern disease, as we can see from some of the most ancient laws.

King Hammurabi (who ruled ancient Babylon in 1800 BC) is best remembered for his 282 laws that were carved on an eight-foot-high stone monument. Although, to our minds, some of these laws were rather brutal – e.g.:

> King Hammurabi's Law Number 21: If one citizen tunnels through the wall of another's house and robs it, then the citizen is sentenced to death. The execution shall take place outside the tunnel and the body shall be used to fill the tunnel.

– they did, nonetheless, mark the beginning of impartial justice. Instead of relying on the arbitrary decision of a ruler or a judge, everyone knew what punishment would be meted out for each crime and they also knew what was and *wasn't* a crime.[1]

This system of laws solved a lot of social problems – there were punishments for criminals and compensation for victims – but they still left a host of difficulties and even created some new ones. For example, it didn't help abandoned women because a man was still allowed to walk out on his wife and children at any time without having to leave her any money or property or pay her any maintenance. In fact the law actually made things worse for her than before because it said that if her husband came back he could reclaim her and the children. The Middle Assyrian law (from 1400 BC) was a little more humane than all the other laws of the ancient Near East because it did allow an abandoned wife to be free after five years.[2]

Imagine that you are a wife in the time of Moses or before. Your husband goes off with some friends to a market in another town and his friends return without him. They report that he has fallen for a pretty young woman. Later on they bring you a message from him that he isn't coming back, but saying that you can keep the children and stay in the house he built… and good luck! This isn't very comforting and it's only the beginning of your nightmare. If you don't find work, your family will soon starve and freeze. If you have enough land around the house for crops and sheep it's possible to grow food, spin wool, and barter for other goods, but all this is very hard work, especially for a single mother.

Unless you have grown sons who are strong enough to work the land (without the help of tractors and weed-killer) you have very few choices. There are few professions for women so you either have to go back to your parents' home (if they are still alive) or you have to get married again so that your new husband can work the land and teach your sons. It's very difficult, however, for you to get remarried when the law says that your original husband can reclaim you at any time and that he can also reclaim your children. He might wait till your children have become economically useful workers and then decide to enforce his rights. This means that your new husband would lose you and his step-children whom he'd spent several years supporting, feeding and training. Any man who married you would have to accept this as a very real possibility and so your chances of finding a new husband are very small.

## Moses makes things better

The one place where the law was fairer for abandoned women was Israel. The Ten Commandments came with many other laws which amplified these basic rules. This new code was a remarkable one and was more enlightened than any others in the ancient Near East.

For example, in Hammurabi's code, people were not considered to be equal. If you hurt an *ordinary* person you had to pay a fine, but if the person was *important* you were punished by being given equal injury.[3]

According to the laws given to Moses, however, if you injured someone it didn't matter what their rank was. Whoever it was, you were punished by being given the same injury you had given to them – 'Eye for eye, tooth for tooth' (Ex. 21.24). This was the same punishment that was given under Hammurabi's law for harming a high-ranking official. In other words, everyone in Israel was treated with equal respect – and they were all treated as though they were important. (For the modern reader, of course, this level of punishment seems barbaric, but it *was* appropriate for the time – especially when compared with punishments in surrounding nations which were often extremely gruesome.[4])

The most impressive differences between the laws of Israel and other ancient Near Eastern nations were in the laws of remarriage. In other countries it was difficult for an abandoned woman to get remarried, but in Israel this unfairness was corrected by giving her the right to receive a divorce certificate from her husband.

> Deut. 24.1: ...he writes her a certificate of divorce and puts it in her hand and sends her out of his house.

This certificate had to be given to any woman who was abandoned or thrown out by her husband. It confirmed that her husband had divorced her and meant that it was safe for another man to marry her – he didn't have to worry that her first husband would return one day to demand his wife back.

## Equality under the Law of Moses

In fact, Israelite women were not the only women in the ancient Near East to be given the right to have such a certificate. Some privileged wives of high-ranking army officers were given a similar certificate if their husbands were missing and presumed dead after a battle. Without a body it was uncertain if the husband was really dead and so the wife was not able to remarry – however long he was missing. But the Middle Assyrian law made a special concession for such a wife so that after waiting for two years without news of her husband, she was given a "certificate of widowhood". This contained the words, "You are now free to marry any man you wish." The same words as these are found in all of the Jewish divorce certificates that have survived from the earliest times, and we can therefore presume that these certificates were patterned on something like this ancient concession for war widows of high-ranking officers.[5]

All Israelites shared an equally high rank in Moses' law, so it wasn't just high-ranking women who could have this type of certificate but *any* woman whose husband abandoned her. The Law of Moses recognised that our sinfulness can end a marriage and it made sure that women didn't suffer more than could be helped. I also expect that this process of writing out a divorce certificate made a lot of men think again and possibly stopped them taking the wrong decision.

The fact that Israelite women could be given a divorce certificate doesn't mean that God thinks divorce is a good idea. He designed marriage to last for ever – for both the couple's and the children's benefit – and when a marriage breaks up it is always a disaster. We have learnt that we have to distinguish between marriage break-up, which is always wrong, and divorce, which is the legal recognition that a marriage *has* broken up. Moses' law did not say that it was acceptable to break up a marriage; it merely prescribed the legal process which was necessary *after* the break-up has happened. It said that the man can't have his cake and eat it; he can't abandon his wife and expect her to be waiting for him at a later date. Whatever sin causes the marriage to break up, there should be a clean end. Neither partner should hold the other as a prisoner in a marriage which is dead.

## Are marriages any better today?

At first glance, the teaching on divorce in the New Testament is very different from the Old Testament teaching (though we will find in later chapters that this is not quite the case). If it *were* very different, it would suggest that marriage or humanity had changed, so that we needed different laws.

Unfortunately the world has not changed much with regard to marriage, because just as many marriages break down now as in Biblical times. The true extent of marriage break-up in the modern world was not recognised until the divorce laws were liberalised and, although easier divorce means that some people get divorced unnecessarily, no-one divorces when they are happily married. The New Testament world and the modern world have just as many instances of broken marriage vows because they both suffer the same human sinfulness as in the ancient Near East.

In the Roman Empire of New Testament times, divorce was very common. People married when they were young and, as the years went by, they were likely to feel differently about each other. It was easy to get divorced and the law did nothing to discourage it. One partner could just walk out on a marriage without any need to divide up the property or provide maintenance for the children. Things are a little different today because compulsory financial arrangements help to support the partner who brings up the children, but our society is becoming more and more similar to the Roman society of the 1st century because fewer couples are getting married, so that either partner can simply walk out of the relationship, just like they could walk out of their relationship in Roman law.

## To conclude: God's law in an imperfect world

The world which God made, including marriage, was perfect and wonderful, but everything was spoiled when we rebelled and became selfish. God told Adam and Eve that as a result of their sin, growing food would become difficult and there would be problems in the relationships between men and women (Gen. 3.16–19). Many harvests failed and many marriages too. When marriages failed, the woman, being more vulnerable, usually suffered. The Law of Moses limited the damage which divorce inflicts by forcing men to give their ex-wife a certificate that allowed them to remarry.

In the next chapter, we will see that the laws of the Old Testament have even more to say on the subject of a broken marriage and that it is always on the side of the victim, whether it is the man or the woman.

## Further Reading

*Origin and wording of the Jewish divorce certificate*

The middle of Chapter 2 "The Pentateuch" in my *Divorce and Remarriage in the Bible* (Eerdmans, 2002) summarises most of the data.

My article "Deuteronomy 24.1–4 and the Origin of the Jewish Divorce Certificate" (*Journal of Jewish Studies* 49, 1998, 230–243) has more details.

*Ancient Near Eastern law codes and the Old Testament*

Chapter 2 "The Pentateuch" in my *Divorce and Remarriage in the Bible* (Eerdmans, 2002) compares the Law of Moses with other ancient Near Eastern law codes.

*Ancient Near Eastern texts relating to the Old Testament (ANET)* edited by James B. Pritchard (Princeton University Press, c.1978, 1992) contains virtually all the texts, except for a few recent discoveries.

*Old Testament Parallels: Laws and Stories from the Ancient Near East* by Victor H. Matthews and Don. C. Benjamin (Paulist Press, 1991, 1997) selects the most important examples and gives short introductions.

*The modern situation and how we got here*

*Road to Divorce, England 1530–1987* by Lawrence Stone (Oxford University Press, 1990) is a highly academic book though it is made easy to read by a multitude of real-life stories from the past.

"The Changing Face of Marriage and Divorce" by Greg Forster (*Anvil* 17, 2000, 167–178) gives a quick review of all the relevant statistics for the UK.

*The Great Divorce Controversy* by Edward S. Williams (Belmont House Publishing, 2000) analyses the social trends and divorce legislation of the UK especially for the last few decades. He also tries to contribute to the Biblical debate but does this much less well.

# 3

# God the Reluctant Divorcee

## God's marriage contract and the grounds for his divorce from Israel

The following is *not* a true story! A man (let's call him Fred) went to a cheese and wine function where he was cornered by a church minister wearing a very tall clerical collar. Fred was nervous and mumbled to the minister that he wasn't really a religious person. Unfortunately this appeared to make the minister even more interested in him, so Fred was relieved when they were interrupted by a lady with a tray of drinks. Gratefully, Fred took a glass, but then the minister sniffed the tray suspiciously and said to the lady in an embarrassingly loud voice: "I would rather commit adultery than drink alcohol!" Poor Fred, realising that he had done something wrong but not sure what it was, put the drink back on the tray and said: "I'm very sorry – I didn't know there was a choice."

We can laugh at this because adultery is so much a normal part of modern life. We are aghast when some countries punish adultery with imprisonment or even the death penalty, but in the ancient Near East adultery was always a capital offence and often the husband was expected to carry out the punishment. Even suspected adultery resulted in a trial by ordeal in the Temple. The woman had to drink a special mixture which supposedly only harmed the guilty (see the details in Num. 5). In much of the ancient world adultery was regarded as seriously as murder and although we may not put adultery in the same bracket as murder today, it can certainly kill a marriage.

## 'Thou shalt not commit adultery'

In the Old Testament if someone was found to have committed adultery their punishment was not always the death penalty, but it did result in the death of a marriage.

Deut. 24.1: When a man takes a wife and marries her, if then she finds
no favour in his eyes because he has found some indecency in her... he
writes her a certificate of divorce and puts it in her hand and sends her
out of his house...

The words "some indecency" in this text could be more literally
translated "a thing of nakedness" or "a cause of sexual immorality"[6]
and it most likely refers to "adultery". Some say that this sexual
immorality could not have been 'adultery' because adulterers were
killed (Lev. 20.10), however the death penalty was not always carried
out since Old Testament law was not applied uniformly throughout
its history. This is God's lovingly realistic way of dealing with the
consequences of human sinfulness: the victim of adultery should
have the choice of whether to end the marriage or not.

Adultery is not, of course, the only sin that can end a marriage.
Many marriages are killed by neglect or abuse. Christians today
accept that the Bible allows divorce for     adultery but often believe
that it does not allow divorce for reasons such as physical or emotional abuse; or when a man withholds money from his wife, or
stops her going out; or when a wife neglects the children and
leaves them filthy and starving. This has led to Christians feeling
confused and concerned because they conclude that God isn't
interested in such things; these issues don't seem to touch his
heart. But why? Why is adultery a more valid reason for divorce
than cruelty? Why *wouldn't* God allow divorce in these situations?
And why wouldn't a victim be allowed, at the very least, the
choice of being able to leave such a marriage?

## Three more Biblical grounds for divorce

In fact, the Bible *does* have a law which addresses this situation.
Exodus 21.10–11 is a text which is usually forgotten, but it provides
precisely what is needed because it allows the victim of abuse or neglect to be freed from the marriage.

This text is actually a law about a slave who has married her master, and states the rights which she has if he decides to marry a second wife. This law tells him to make sure that he doesn't neglect his
first wife when he marries a second.

Ex. 21.10–11: If he takes another wife to himself, he shall not diminish
her food, her clothing, or her conjugal love. And if he does not do these

three things for her, she shall go out for nothing, without payment of money. [7]

At first glance this text doesn't seem to apply to us at all – because we don't have second wives and we don't marry slaves (though in some marriages it might seem like it!) – but we will see that actually it applies to *all* marriages.

Polygamy was allowed in the Old Testament and when a man took a second wife he often neglected his first wife (human nature being what it is) and favoured the new one. This was especially likely if his first wife had been a slave before he married her and so the point of this law was to ensure that the first wife was treated fairly. It says that the husband would not be permitted to withhold food, clothing or conjugal love from her. If he did neglect any of these she would be able to go free – that is, she could get divorced.

Before we dismiss this as irrelevant to our marriages today it is important to remember that this is case law, not statute law, which means that the principles are more important than the details. Then, as now, some laws were written as 'statutes' which summarise a whole subject area (such as 'Divorce'), and some laws were 'case law'. Case law is a collection of decisions made by judges in actual cases which established a new legal principle. These rulings can then be applied to other cases which share something in common with the case which established the principle. For example, the statute law on keeping the Sabbath is part of the Ten Commandments (Ex. 20.8–11), though these did not define the punishment for breaking it. When a man was caught gathering sticks on a Sabbath (Num. 15.32–36) they brought his case before Moses who decided that he deserved death. This story, with the decision about the punishment, became an item of case law – the principle which was derived from it is that breaking the Sabbath law is liable to the death penalty.

Exodus 21.10–11 is case law, so we have to ignore the details about slavery and polygamy and look for the *principles* which apply to all marriages which involve neglect. The Rabbis found the following principles in this text and I think they were right. They reasoned that if a *slave* wife had the right to divorce a husband who neglected to supply food, clothing and conjugal love, then a *free* wife would certainly also have this right. And they argued that if one of two wives had this right, then so did an only wife. Furthermore, if a wife had these rights, then a husband was also entitled to the same right to divorce a wife who neglected him. The Biblical principle which is established, therefore, is the right of someone to divorce their partner if they neglect their vow to give you food, clothing or conjugal love.

## Four marriage vows

This means that the Old Testament recognises four grounds for divorce. The first three are neglect of food, clothing and conjugal love (by either husband or wife) and the fourth is committing adultery.

These four obligations were the same as the vows exchanged by couples in Jewish marriages. They promised to feed, clothe, exchange conjugal love and be faithful to each other. The man agreed to provide food and cloth, and the woman agreed to cook and sew, and they both agreed to share conjugal love and be faithful.

Actually, for technical reasons, only a wife could be divorced for adultery because a man could have more than one wife. This did not make it OK for him to commit adultery, but it meant that he could not be divorced for doing so because he had not promised sexual fidelity to his wife alone. Well, that's how some Rabbis argued, although I am not sure I agree. They also said that Deuteronomy 24.1 only spoke about adultery by a woman, but Deuteronomy 24.1–4 is another example of case law, so principles are more important than the details, and the principle is that adultery is a ground for divorce. Jesus put an end to this loophole by teaching monogamy, so that adultery became an equal ground for divorce for both sexes – but I will leave the teaching of Jesus for another chapter.

Therefore, in the Old Testament there were very sensible laws about divorce. Each partner had to keep his or her four marriage vows to feed, clothe, share conjugal love and be faithful. The principles behind these details are that they had to supply material support (food and clothing) and physical affection (conjugal love). Abusive situations were covered by these laws because physical and emotional abuse are extreme forms of neglecting material support or physical affection.

The only person who could choose to enact a divorce was the victim. If your partner broke his or her marriage vows, you could choose to divorce them, or you could choose to forgive them and try to salvage the marriage. You could not divorce a partner simply because you wanted to, although this had changed by the time of Jesus, as we will see later.

## God's divorce

These four Biblical grounds for divorce are illustrated by God's marriage to Israel which ended unhappily in divorce when Israel sinned. Many of the Old Testament prophets speak about the problems in that relationship.

Hosea was told to marry a prostitute who continued to be unfaithful to him, in order to illustrate God's marriage to Israel (Hos. 1–3). Ezekiel described how Israel committed adultery with other gods along with other sins which led to the divorce (Ezek. 16 & 23). Jeremiah warned Israel's sister nation Judah to watch out because she was heading the same way (Jer. 3–4). Isaiah brought the good news that Judah only suffered separation and that God wished for reconciliation, unlike Israel who *was* divorced (Is. 50).

Therefore the Old Testament prophets described God as a divorcee, and when you put together all the references, you find a clear and unanimous picture. God had married Israel at Mount Sinai in the Wilderness, then brought his bride across the threshold of the Jordan into Palestine. There he gave her food (milk and honey) and wool for clothes, and of course he loved her and was faithful to her. But in Palestine, Israel was introduced to many other gods and started to worship them, offering them sacrifices of food and ornaments. The prophets described this worship of other gods as spiritual adultery.

The books of Moses and the historical books describe these same matters in different language; they portray God's relationship with Israel as a treaty contract. The structure of much of the book of Deuteronomy follows the normal structure of a treaty covenant, with an historical prologue (Deut. 1–4), followed by stipulations of the covenant (Deut. 5–26), then the names of divine witnesses (Deut. 4.26; 26.16–19), and ending with blessings and curses (Deut. 27–28). This covenant treaty is just like an ancient Near Eastern treaty where both sides agree on what they will do (the stipulations) and the more powerful side makes promises for when the stipulations are kept and threats for when the stipulations are broken (the blessings and curses). They called this a 'contract' which is often translated as 'covenant', but the two words have the same meaning and there is only one Hebrew word (*berit*) behind them both.

Some people think that a marriage should not be called a 'contract' because it is a 'covenant'. The difference is, they say, that a 'contract' can be broken but a 'covenant' can never end even if the stipulations are constantly being broken. They say that national treaties and trade agreements are 'contracts', but when God makes an agreement with his people it should be called a 'covenant' A 'covenant' is seen pre-eminently in the 'New Covenant' which is made with Judah and Israel (Jer. 31.31), after which the New Testament gets its name.

There are very big problems with this idea, the biggest of which is that 'covenant' and 'contract' are both translations of the same Hebrew word, so the idea of a distinction does not exist in the Bible. Although it is true that the New Covenant is unbreakable and does not rely on keeping the stipulations, this does not mean that every agreement which God makes is like this or that marriage is like this. God's first covenant or contract with Israel which he made at Mount Sinai certainly had stipulations (the Law) and curses and blessings which resulted from breaking or keeping these stipulations. Marriage is also regarded by Malachi as a contract which can be broken, and the prophets regarded God's marriage contract with Israel as breakable.

## A broken contract

An ancient treaty contract and an ancient marriage contract are both similar to a modern commercial contract. Both sides agree to stipulations (e.g. "You build this and I'll pay you") and make promises ("I'll pay you on time if you finish on time") with threats of penalties ("There's a penalty of £1000 if you don't finish on time").

Mrs Hopeful asked Mr Oddjob the builder to build her a conservatory by the end of June. Her daughter was getting married in 8 weeks' time on July 1st and the reception would be held in the lounge and large garden at home. Mr Oddjob was enthusiastic, "No problem, Madam. My price, just for you, is £4000."

"That's a deal," she said, "so long as it's finished by July 1st."

"Don't worry," he assured her, "it'll only take 20 days." But he neglected to say that he would spread the 20 days over three months, and when the wedding day arrived there was nothing but a muddy building site which the guests had to tramp across to get into the garden.

The next day, Mrs Hopeful phoned up Mr Oddjob: "You've broken our contract. I'll pay you £2000 for your work so far, and I'll get someone else to finish the job."

"You can't do that!" he complained. "You agreed a contract for the whole job." And that was just the start of a long story...

Who was in the right? Mrs Hopeful or Mr Oddjob? I think most fair-minded people would agree that Mrs Hopeful had the right to end the contract because the builder broke one of the stipulations which was that he would finish by July 1st (though a good lawyer might win his case by arguing that she did not use the magical legal phrase "time is of the essence"). In our law, as in ancient law, the victim of a broken contract can decide to end it, or they can decide to carry on in the hope that things will get better.

God's contract (or 'covenant') with Israel also had stipulations, promises and penalties. The stipulations were the Ten Commandments and the other laws; the promises were a peaceful life in the Promised Land he had given them; and the penalties were the removal of his protection and exile from that Land. Sadly, as we know, the Israelites broke the Commandments, so God sent them into exile, just as he said he would in the contract.

That is the way the historical books of the OT viewed the exile of Israel – as a broken treaty contract. But the prophets regarded God's relationship with Israel like a marriage contract. This was very similar because it, too, had stipulations, promises and penalties. The stipulations were the vows to feed, clothe and share conjugal love in faithfulness; the promise was a happy life together; and the penalty was divorce. Israel continuously broke these stipulations until God eventually divorced her, and the prophets warned Judah that she was heading the same way. As Jeremiah said:

> Jer. 3.8: Judah saw that for all the adulteries of that faithless one, Israel, I had sent her away with a decree of divorce. Yet her treacherous sister Judah did not fear, but she too went and played the whore.

## Israel's broken marriage vows

Ezekiel was particularly interested in the grounds for God's divorce. He warned Judah that she was going the same way as her sister kingdom of Israel (23.30–33). God kept all four of his marriage vows: he loved Judah, and gave her food and clothing fit for a queen (16.8–13) and of course he was faithful to her. But, in contrast, Judah broke all four marriage vows: she did not return God's love; she committed adultery with idols (16.15); she presented idols with the food which God had given her (16.19); and she decorated idols with the cloth and jewels with which God had honoured her (16.16–18).

God warned Judah that he had already divorced Israel for these types of sins (23.9). The remarkable message of the prophets was that although God had every right to divorce Judah, just as he had divorced her 'sister' Israel, he decided to do something completely different. He decided to create a 'New Covenant' which would transform people from the inside. Unlike all previous covenants, and unlike any human covenant, this one could not be broken when one side failed to keep the stipulations but it would continue unconditionally for ever (16.60–62). These prophecies were fulfilled in the New Testament (which is named after this New Covenant) when Christ died for all sin. Even Israel was going to share in this restoration, not by remarrying God, but by rejoining Judah to become a single new nation (Ezek. 37:15–28).

Israel did not know anything about God's wonderful future plans while she was heading for divorce, and yet she stubbornly continued to break her marriage vows. All the prophets portray God acting in a forgiving and patient manner – he didn't divorce her immediately and gave her many chances to repent. But Israel, his wife, continued to sin, refusing to honour her vows and God reluctantly had to divorce her. The marriage was broken and dead, and God merely carried out the legal formalities of divorce which recognised that fact.

## God hates divorce

We know now why God says in Malachi that he "hates divorce",[8] because he knows from personal experience how much pain results from it. As he says in Malachi, divorce results from breaking marriage contract promises – promises which God himself was a witness to.

> Mal. 2.14: The Lord was witness between you and the wife of your youth, to whom you have been faithless, though she is your companion and your wife by covenant.

God does not criticise the legal process of divorce, or the person who carries it out – otherwise he would criticise himself, because he had to divorce Israel. God hates the breaking of marriage vows which *result* in divorce. He says that breaking these vows is being "faithless" because it breaks the marriage "covenant" or "contract". Marriages are ended by the person who breaks the marriage vows – not by the innocent person who decides to end the broken contract by enacting a divorce. Divorce is usually terrible for both partners, but remaining married can often be worse. Suffering continued neglect or abuse can be physically and emotionally damaging, and continuing unfaithfulness can bring the whole institution of marriage into disrepute.

## To conclude: Practical laws for a sinful world

We have seen that in the Old Testament marriage is a contract, so it can be ended if one party breaks the stipulations which were agreed in it, but the only person who has the right to end a contract is the victim of broken promises. They can decide to continue or they can decide that enough is enough. The Old Testament therefore gives us some very practical laws on divorce. A person cannot divorce their husband or wife simply because they want to, but only if their spouse had broken their marriage vows. Divorce is not compulsory; the innocent partner also has the choice to forgive and carry on in the marriage.

Imagine the situation if Mrs Hopeful had married Mr Oddjob instead of employing him. They promised to feed, clothe, share conjugal love and be faithful to each other. And imagine what would happen if he started hitting her or spending all the housekeeping money. Would she have the right to end the marriage contract? Under Old Testament law – yes. Or imagine what would happen if she started taking lovers and spending his money on them. Would he have the right to divorce her? Under Old Testament law – yes.

In the sad reality of this world, a marriage contract or covenant can most certainly be broken by a partner who breaks their marriage vows. The Old Testament is aware of human sin, and has practical laws to deal with its consequences, and we will see that there is nothing to suggest that the New Testament is any less practical. We will see in chapter 5 that Jesus recognises the necessity of divorce, but says that we should avoid it whenever possible.

## Further Reading

### On the three grounds in Exodus 21.10–11

The second half of chapter 1 "The Ancient Near East" in my *Divorce and Remarriage in the Bible* (Eerdmans, 2002) deals with this text in the ancient Near Eastern context.

The middle section of chapter 5 "Rabbinic teaching" in my *Divorce and Remarriage in the Bible* (Eerdmans, 2002) deals with the way that the Jews applied this text in their divorce laws.

This text is often recognised by Jewish scholars as the basis for early Jewish divorce laws, but I have only found one Christian who discusses it with regard to NT teaching on divorce: William F. Luck in his *Divorce and Remarriage: Recovering the Biblical View* (Harper and Row, 1987), pp. 31–34.

### On God's divorce in the prophets

Chapter 3 "The Later Prophets" in my *Divorce and Remarriage in the Bible* (Eerdmans, 2002) looks at the prophets in some detail.

My article "Three Weddings and a Divorce: God's Covenant with Israel, Judah and the Church" (*Tyndale Bulletin* 47, 1996, 1–26) looks at the wider picture, including the New Testament church.

Andrew Cornes deals with this very well in his *Divorce and Remarriage: Biblical principles and pastoral practice* (Eerdmans; Hodder & Stoughton, 1993) – though his conclusions are completely opposite to my own.

*Whoredom: God's unfaithful wife in Biblical theology* by Raymond C. Ortlund (Apollos, 1996) covers the whole subject in great detail.

### On ancient Near Eastern treaty covenants

James H. Walton, *Ancient Israelite literature in its cultural context: a survey of parallels between Biblical and ancient Near Eastern texts* (Zondervan, 1989) – chapter 4 is a good summary of the texts and how they compare to the OT.

# 4

# The Church Can't Do Without It

### Jesus criticised those who abandoned Old Testament law

The preceding chapters have shown us that the Old Testament has some very useful and practical things to say about divorce, but we live in the New Testament age, and many people would say that we have to put the Old Testament behind us. It's true that we cannot simply apply the Old Testament law as though nothing has changed, but Jesus called us to take note of every letter of God's law so we cannot simply ignore it.

You may have heard the following story. I had already heard it in Christian circles when a Jewish professor from Jerusalem told it to me as something which actually happened to a friend of his in New York. Perhaps I have found the origin of the story, or perhaps his friend was just passing it on as a good story:

A semi-religious Jewish family went to a new synagogue and their eldest son, Adam, reluctantly attended the Sabbath School. Afterwards, over lunch, his father asked Adam what he had learned. At first he seemed reticent to say anything, but after thinking for a bit he replied enthusiastically:

"We learned about how Moses took his people across the Red Sea and defeated the Egyptians. He lined up his tanks against them, then sent amphibious craft onto the Red Sea to start building a pontoon. When it was finished the Israelites all ran across while their fighter planes gave them cover. The Egyptians chased them, but Moses blew up the pontoon and the Egyptians all drowned."

"Now, Adam," said his father, "I'm sure that's not what the teacher told you!"

"Well, no – not quite," admitted Adam, "but if I told you what he really said, you'd never believe it!"

## Applying the Old Testament today

The Old Testament is just too old for some people. The culture it was addressing is now ancient and the laws it contains are largely unworkable today. No-one today can imagine putting a suspected adulteress through a life-threatening ordeal to see if she is guilty or not (as in Num. 5), or treating a woman as unclean for 40 days after she has given birth to a boy, or 80 days if it is a girl (as in Lev. 12). We do not sell our children as slaves (as at the start of Ex. 21), or buy foreign slaves and leave them to our children in our wills (as in Lev. 25.44–46).

Our culture is very different now – thanks largely to the effect of the Gospel – and many of these Old Testament laws no longer apply. Even some New Testament ethics are now out of date, because no Christian leader would send a slave back to his owner like Paul did with Onesimus, even if they sent him with a letter which was as wise and culturally transforming as the letter Paul sent to Philemon. And although some churches still insist that women keep their heads covered in church, the reason for this is no longer a question of common decency as it was in the days of the New Testament, when uncovering your hair was equivalent to wearing a bikini or less.

Despite the cultural changes, however, believers today would not think of putting aside the whole New Testament, but some Christians do act as though the whole Old Testament can be ignored.

## The moral and ceremonial laws

There are three main ways by which we can decide what parts of the Old Testament laws still apply to Christians today. The most common method is to say that the New Testament has left behind the ceremonial laws (such as sacrifices, food laws and cleanliness issues), while it has inherited the moral laws (such as the Ten Commandments and the other moral demands of Moses and the prophets). The rationale for this difference can be based on the death of Christ because the ceremonial law was completely fulfilled by his sacrifice.

This tidy division between moral and ceremonial law is a good rule-of-thumb but it is sometimes difficult to know into which category each law fits. For example, many believers would regard tithing as a moral principle, although very few apply the Old Testament details about tithing one tenth for religious workers (the Levites, as in Num. 18.20–24) and a second tenth for celebrating religious festivals and for the poor (as prescribed in Deut. 14.22–29). Similarly the details of punishments for disobeying moral principles should also be ignored, such as the punishing of "eye for eye" or executing a rebellious son who is a glutton and drunkard (see Deut. 21.18–21).

Another method is to say that Christians should follow the moral principles in the Old Testament but not the *details* – the quantities, dates and punishments which belong to a former age. As we will see, Jesus applied the principles rather than the details of Old Testament law, so this method could be said to be following his example.

A third method is to say that Christians should ignore any Old Testament laws which are not specifically mentioned in the New Testament. This is an argument from silence which, as we will see in chapter 7, should only be used when the silence is surprising. For example, it is not surprising that the New Testament should fail to repeat every moral command contained in the Old Testament, because the Old Testament is much longer than the New Testament and because it has a lot more passages relating to moral behaviour. Therefore most Christians conclude that we have inherited all the Old Testament moral principles which are not specifically *denied* in the New Testament.

The two Testaments are also different in style, because the Old Testament contains mainly laws and commands, whereas the New Testament contains mainly moral guidelines and exhortations. This is due to the fact that the Old Testament was largely written by lawmakers and prophets for the guidance of a nation, whereas the New Testament was written for churches and individual believers who needed guidance about how to live within the laws of whatever nation they found themselves in. This difference has made some people think that the religion of the Old Testament is legalistic and mainly concerned with punishment, while the New Testament is full of grace and forgiveness. This is nonsense, of course, because God has not changed: he was no less forgiving in the Old Testament than he is now, though the basis of his forgiveness (the death of Jesus) is a New Testament event.

It is ironic that the New Testament, which emphasises God's grace and forgiveness, is usually regarded as much harsher with regard to victims of marital abuse. The traditional interpretation assumes that Jesus introduced a new and stricter policy which overturned the Old Testament principle that a victim has the right to bring their suffering to an end. But if we examine Jesus' attitude to the Old Testament we find that he had a very high regard for it, so we would not expect him to overturn one of its important moral principles.

## Jesus' view of the Old Testament

Jesus regarded the Old Testament as God's Word and said that every letter was important.

> Mt. 5.17: "Do not think that I have come to abolish the Law or the Prophets; I have not come to abolish them but to fulfil them. [18] For truly, I say to you, until heaven and earth pass away, not an iota, not a dot, will pass from the Law until all is accomplished. [19] Therefore whoever relaxes one of the least of these commandments and teaches others to do the same will be called least in the kingdom of heaven, but whoever does them and teaches them will be called great in the kingdom of heaven."

Jesus fulfilled the ceremonial parts of the law on the cross but he wants *us* to fulfil the moral parts of the law, and he even said that he wanted us to be perfect like our Father (Mt. 5.48). He never told anyone to break an Old Testament law and even though the Pharisees accused him and his disciples of breaking the law, they only broke traditions which the Pharisees had *added* to the Old Testament.

In Matthew 5, where some people think that Jesus overturned Old Testament laws, he actually did the reverse: he affirmed the principles of these laws and *widened* their application. He made a distinction between the original law and the new interpretations by which that law had been changed, and while rejecting the new interpretations, he affirmed the original old law.

vv. 21–26 affirmed the law against murder and applied its principle by saying that if murder which arises from hatred is wrong, then murderous hatred is also wrong.

vv. 27–30 affirmed the law against adultery by saying that if adultery comes from illicit lust, then illicit lust is wrong. And if illicit lust comes from lustful looking, then lustful looking is also wrong.

vv. 31–32 affirmed the law of divorce in Deuteronomy 24.1, which we will look at more closely, especially in chapter 5.

vv. 33–37 affirmed the law against making false oaths to God, saying that if it was wrong to lie to God, then it is wrong to speak *any* lies.

vv. 38–42 affirmed the Old Testament limitations to the laws of compensation (i.e. if someone knocked your tooth out, your revenge may not be greater than knocking his tooth out) by saying that if the law tells us to restrict our wish for revenge, then we should avoid revenge altogether.

vv. 43–47 affirmed the law to love your neighbour and rejected the words "and hate your enemy" which some people had added to this command.

### Jesus highlighted principles, not details

As well as endorsing these laws, Jesus amplified them by identifying the principles behind them and applying those principles to the whole of life. The principle behind "You shall not murder" and "You shall not commit adultery" is to avoid the causes of these sins, as well as the sins themselves. The principle behind the importance of honesty in oaths and loving one's neighbour is that these attitudes should encompass the whole of life, so that all our statements are honest, and all our relationships, even with our enemies, are governed by love.

Jesus never criticised what the Old Testament said, though he frequently criticised the way people interpreted it. He condemned the way that some people tried to side-step the command about oaths by claiming that they were not making a real oath if they swore 'by Heaven' or 'by Jerusalem' (vv. 34–35), and he criticised the way that people had diluted the command to "Love your neighbour" by saying that this did not include enemies. And, as we will see in chapter 5, Jesus reproved those who wrongly interpreted an Old Testament ruling about divorce so that they could invent a new ground for divorce.

It is clear, then, that Jesus did not reject the Old Testament, but he did reject the new interpretations which had diluted the Old Testament's moral principles. He emphasised the importance of the Old Testament law by saying:

> Mt. 5.19: "Whoever relaxes one of the least of these commandments and teaches others to do the same will be called least in the kingdom of heaven."

Jesus did not mean that we should keep all the *details* of Old Testament law in exactly the way it was prescribed for the nation of Israel in the ancient Near Eastern world. We can see from the way that he discussed these various commandments in Matthew 5 that he was concerned with the *principles* behind the laws rather than the details, and therefore we can also legitimately ignore the details of Old Testament law, but we may not neglect any of the *principles*.

Occasionally we can ignore a few Old Testament principles, such as laws about how to treat our slaves, because (thank God) most countries are now free of this scourge. But this does not give us a reason to ignore the principles about divorce, because the world of marriage and sexual relations has not changed very much. Jesus taught that Old Testament moral principles should be applied much more strictly by Christians – not *less*.

## The basis of modern laws

Many of the laws forming the basis of our modern legal systems and Christian ethics only occur in the Old Testament. Without the Old Testament, in fact, the Bible would have no word of criticism for either rape or consensual sex outside marriage. These are dealt with in Deuteronomy 22.23–29 with clarity and fairness, though the degrees of punishment would not be appropriate in modern societies.

Many other branches of modern law are not only illustrated by the Old Testament, but are established on the principles which were inspired by Old Testament law. Our forefathers had a very high regard for God's law, and they did not reject its principles simply because they were not found in the New Testament.

One chapter in particular, Exodus 21, has provided the foundations for our modern laws on murder and injury. It established the differences between accidental killing, unpremeditated murder, and premeditated murder (vv. 21.12–14) – categories which are at the heart of murder laws in most modern societies. Our laws of injury and compensation are based on the principle that recompense should reflect the amount of damage done (vv. 23–25), and on the different categories of deliberate harm, accidental harm and consequential harm which are defined in this chapter (vv. 18–22). This same chapter also established principles about accidental harm by animals under someone's care and made a distinction between foreseeable injury and unforeseeable accidents, with higher fines for those who had not taken the necessary precautions (v. 29). Although modern law has multiplied the details into bewildering complexities, the foundations are still recognisable in Exodus 21.

Exodus 21 is also where we find the moral principle that a victim of marital neglect or abuse can choose to end the marriage. Bearing in mind that other principles in the same passage form the foundation of our national laws, we should therefore think very carefully before we choose simply to dismiss it. Likewise the church should not decide to teach the Old Testament morals about sex outside marriage and yet reject its morals about neglect or abuse within marriage.

## To conclude: Keeping the spirit of the Law

God has given us his laws to help us in a practical way. Imagine what would happen if God's marriage laws were kept without exception for just one generation – all the sexually transmitted diseases would be wiped out for ever! So as well as providing a model for the world of the ancient Near East, the Old Testament law also provides a model for our modern world – because human nature has not changed very much!

In the following chapters we will look at what the New Testament says about the specific Old Testament law concerning the victim of marital neglect or abuse. As I have mentioned, some interpreters say that Jesus' teaching brought the Old Testament law about divorce to an end, but we will see in the following chapters that Jesus and Paul actually *affirmed* it, and that Jesus criticised the Pharisees for changing it.

## Further Reading

### On the Old Testament in relation to the New

*Two Testaments, One Bible: a study of the theological relationship between the Old and New Testaments* (Apollos, 1991) by David Baker, who emphasises the intrinsic links between both Testaments.

*Christ and the Bible* by John Wenham (Baker, 1994) shows how Jesus regarded the Old Testament as real history.

*The Institutes of Biblical Law* by R.J. Rushdoony, (Presbyterian & Reformed Publishing Co., 1973) tries to apply virtually all the Old Testament to Christian lifestyle. This is an extreme example of using the Old Testament, but it is interesting to see how much he can achieve.

# 5

# Divorce on Demand?

**Jesus taught us to forgive the repentant partner**

A man in Dubai divorced his wife in 2001 by a totally new method – he sent her a text message on her phone. She had failed to turned up on time to cook his tea, so he texted her: "You're late. I divorce you." This was the third time he'd told her he would divorce her and according to Islamic law if a man tells his wife "I divorce you" three times, this is all that is needed: the wife is legally divorced when she receives that third message. The woman in Dubai could not believe that she could be divorced by a text message so she took it to the Muslim court, but the court upheld the man's right. Any Muslim man is allowed to divorce his wife in this way without needing to show that she has done anything wrong. A Muslim woman, however, is not allowed to divorce her husband at all.

## A new type of divorce, for men only

Jewish men are also able to get a divorce quite easily without needing to cite any grounds. Instead of saying 'I divorce you' three times, a Jewish man has to write out a divorce certificate, give it to his wife and as soon as she receives it, she is legally divorced. As in Islamic law, only men can initiate divorce and it is a groundless divorce because the man does not have to show that his wife has done anything wrong. The groundless divorce also means that the woman cannot defend herself.

Although the divorce certificate is part of the law of Moses in Deuteronomy 24.1, this groundless divorce for 'men-only' did not become available until about the time of Jesus' birth. Before this, both Jewish men and women could divorce partners who broke their marriage obligations, as defined in the Old Testament. We also saw in chapter 3 that the OT only allowed the innocent partner to initiate a divorce. If a woman did not feed, clothe or share conjugal love with her husband faithfully, he could divorce her and, likewise, if a man did not give his wife money for food or clothing and did not share conjugal love with her then she could divorce him. These grounds for divorce (based on Ex. 21.10–11) were in use until about AD 70, but by the time that Jesus was preaching, in about AD 30, they were already being used only rarely. During Jesus' lifetime the new groundless divorce gradually grew in popularity until, by about the end of the 1st century, it had totally replaced divorces based on OT grounds.

This new type of divorce was invented by a Rabbi called Hillel (who lived a few decades before Jesus) and was called the 'Any Cause' divorce after the phrase which inspired it in Deuteronomy 24.1 where a man divorced his wife for "a cause of sexual immorality".

> Deut. 24.1: When a man takes a wife and marries her, if then she finds no favour in his eyes because he has found a cause of sexual immorality in her, ...he writes her a certificate of divorce... [9]

Hillel asked the question: Why did Moses use the phrase "cause of sexual immorality" when he could simply have said "sexual immorality"? Hillel reasoned that the seemingly superfluous word "cause" must refer to another, different, ground for divorce and since this other ground is simply called a "cause", he concluded that it meant '*Any* Cause'.[10]

## The 'Any Cause' divorce

Hillel therefore thought that two types of divorce were taught in Deuteronomy 24.1: one for 'Sexual Immorality' (i.e. adultery) and one for 'Any Cause'.

The Hillelite Rabbis came to two main conclusions about the new 'Any Cause' form of divorce. Firstly, they concluded that an 'Any Cause' divorce could only be carried out by men (because the example case in Deuteronomy 24.1 involves a man who divorces his wife). Secondly, they said that it could be used for *any* cause – such as your wife burning a meal – so although the 'Any Cause' divorce was theoretically based on some kind of fault, this fault could be such a small thing that it was, in effect, a groundless divorce.

The 'Any Cause' type of divorce soon became very popular – especially because you didn't need any proof and you didn't have to present your case in court. There was no need to try to prove in court that your wife had neglected you – a very embarrassing process because all your neighbours would find out the details which you had been hiding from them for years! All you needed to do to carry out an 'Any Cause' divorce was write out a divorce certificate and give it to your wife.

The only times when the 'Any Cause' divorce was not more beneficial for the man were those few occasions when he could *prove* that his wife had been unfaithful – and especially when this unfaithfulness became public knowledge. He could get his revenge on his wife by taking her to court to obtain a divorce on the Old Testament ground of unfaithfulness. There was also a financial advantage for the man in this situation because if he could prove that his wife was unfaithful, he did not have to give her the marriage inheritance (the *Ketubah*) which he had promised to her when they married.

Despite the disadvantages to them, many women were also in favour of the 'Any Cause' divorce, because it meant they would probably be able to claim their marriage inheritance (which, in many cases, was large enough to live on). If a wife was taken to court on the OT grounds of being neglectful or abusive, she ran the risk of financial penury because the court could decide to remove some or all of her marriage inheritance from her. A court hearing also, of course, meant public shame and humiliation.

Very soon the 'Any Cause' divorce had almost completely replaced the traditional Old Testament types of divorce. We can see how respectable it had become by the time of Jesus' birth because Joseph considered using this means to break off his betrothal to Mary.

Mt. 1.19: Her husband Joseph, being a just man and unwilling to put her to shame, resolved to divorce her quietly.

Joseph did not want to put Mary through the disgrace of a public trial so he decided to use the quiet 'Any Cause' divorce because it did not require any proof of wrong-doing. Matthew considered that this would be the action of a "just man" because Joseph could have ensured that he didn't have to pay Mary's marriage inheritance if he had decided to prove her guilty of adultery in court.

## "Nothing except 'Sexual Immorality'"

Not everyone accepted this new type of divorce. The disciples of Shammai (a rival of Hillel's who often disagreed with him) said that Hillel had interpreted the Scriptures wrongly and that the whole phrase "a cause of sexual immorality" meant nothing more than the ground of "Sexual Immorality" – it did not mean two grounds, 'Sexual Immorality' *and* 'Any Cause'. They summarised their opinion by saying that, on the basis of Deuteronomy 24.1:

> "A man should not divorce his wife except he has found 'Sexual Immorality' in her."[11]

The interpretation of this short phrase "a cause of sexual immorality" was a matter of huge public debate. The disciples of Shammai wanted people to restrict themselves to divorces based on the Old Testament grounds – unfaithfulness in Deuteronomy 24.1 and neglect of food, clothing or conjugal love in Exodus 21.10–11. But the common people preferred Hillel's interpretation which added the new 'Any Cause' divorce.

The ordinary people were not too interested in the intricate arguments over these interpretations, but because divorce was common in 1st-century Judaism, they nonetheless had to know the basics of the debate so that they could pick the right lawyers. Most people would have had a friend or relative who had been through a divorce and they would therefore have known that Hillel allowed 'Any Cause' divorces and that Shammai said that "a cause of sexual immorality" meant nothing except divorce for 'Sexual Immorality'. In the same way, nowadays, when divorce is also very common, most people recognise legal jargon like 'maintenance payments' and 'access' without necessarily understanding their detailed meanings.

## Asking Jesus' opinion

Therefore, by the time of Jesus, almost every divorce was an 'Any Cause' divorce but the Rabbis were still arguing about it. These rabbis decided to ask Jesus what he thought:

> Mt. 19.3: Is it lawful to divorce one's wife for 'Any Cause'?

This verse is normally translated "Is it lawful to divorce one's wife for any cause" or "...for any reason". As I mentioned in chapter 1, when I was re-reading these familiar words with the benefit of my Rabbinic studies, I found that I was understanding the text differently. This was because I remembered that the Hillelites called their new form of divorce the 'Any Cause' divorce – a legal term which was used by other Jews such as Philo and Josephus as well as by the Rabbis themselves.[12] Identifying this term was not my own new discovery – because many people had already written a great deal about the Hillelite divorce – though this fact had never been taken into account by any of the Biblical translations.

According to the standard translations such as "Is it lawful to divorce one's wife for any cause", the Pharisees appear to be asking Jesus if he thought divorce itself was lawful or not. But the question, "is it lawful to divorce?" is an illogical one because to the Jews 'divorce' means "the procedure which is defined in the law of Moses" – and the law of Moses cannot be 'unlawful'! However, if you translate the question, "Is it lawful to divorce one's wife for 'Any Cause'?" it makes perfect sense. The Rabbis wanted to know what Jesus thought about the new 'Any Cause' type of divorce and how he interpreted Deuteronomy 24.1.

Actually in the account of this episode in Mark, the Rabbis *do* appear to ask the illogical version of the question, "Is it lawful for a man to divorce his wife?" (Mk. 10.2). There is a simple explanation for this: anyone reading Mark in the 1st century would have mentally added, "...for 'Any Cause'" to complete the question because everyone at the time was talking about it. It was like someone today who asks, "Is it lawful for a 16-year-old to drink?" This is an illogical question because, without anything to drink, we dehydrate and die. Therefore we mentally add "...alcoholic beverages" to the end of the question to make sense of it, though it would be pedantic to actually ask the question in this form. In exactly the same way a 1st-century Jew would mentally have added "...for Any Cause" to the end of the otherwise illogical question in Mark 10.

## Understanding the jargon

The account of this debate with the Pharisees is highly abbreviated because it had to fit into a short book. This was the same throughout the Gospels where speeches are shortened to a couple of sentences and fascinating incidents – which might otherwise be recounted as a book in themselves – are recorded in just one paragraph.

These shortened accounts did not matter for a 1st-century Jew, who knew the context and the Old Testament very well, but they sometimes make things a little obscure for a modern reader. Therefore we have to work hard at unpacking the abbreviated account of what Jesus and the Pharisees said. Although superfluous phrases like "for Any Cause" were usually omitted, Matthew decided to state the question in full in order to help his readers because he was writing his Gospel a little later than Mark, when this Rabbinic debate had become less well known.

Jesus was asked if he agreed with the new Hillelite 'Any Cause' divorce, but he wasn't really interested in this debate and was more concerned to tell the Hillelites and Shammaites where they had both gone wrong (as we will see below). When the Rabbis eventually got Jesus back to their question, he gave the same straightforward interpretation of Deuteronomy 24.1 which Shammai taught – that is, he said that the phrase "a cause of sexual immorality" meant "nothing except 'Sexual Immorality'". And, to emphasise this, Jesus said that if someone got divorced on the basis of any other interpretation (i.e. the 'Any Cause' divorce), then they were not properly divorced and so, if they remarried, they would be committing adultery (Mt. 19.9).

Most interpreters have not recognised that Jesus is quoting the Rabbinic legal phrases "divorce for 'Any Cause'" and "nothing except 'Sexual Immorality'". As a result they think that Jesus was asked "Is it ever lawful to divorce?" and that he answered "No – except for sexual immorality".

These interpreters did not know the meaning of the Rabbinic legal phrase "nothing except 'Sexual Immorality'", so they tried to find out what 'sexual immorality' meant by looking carefully at the Greek word (*porneia*). Some interpreted it as 'adultery', and others as 'sex before marriage' (especially during betrothal) or as 'incest'. These definitions are actually *all* correct because *porneia* is a very general word which means all these things as well as any other type of sexual immorality, including visiting prostitutes (as in 1 Cor. 6.13–18). Jesus (or his translator) used it because it was the best translation of the Hebrew word for general 'sexual immorality' (*ervah*) in the Rabbinic legal phrase "except 'Sexual Immorality'".

Jesus was using the same language as the people he was speaking to and he was referring to the same Biblical texts and legal discussions which they all knew about. He was not speaking a new language which only he knew, so we should not ask ourselves what *Jesus* meant by *porneia*, but what his *hearers* or the original *readers* would understand by *porneia* or by the phrase "except for 'Sexual Immorality'". This raises the whole question of how God communicates through

Scripture to a multitude of generations, which we will look at in chapter 12.

## Answering their question

Jesus was answering their question in plain language, and he wasn't making a universal statement. Therefore, when he said "nothing except 'Sexual Immorality'" he was saying that the phrase "a cause of sexual immorality" did not include the extra ground of 'Any Cause', and he didn't mean "there is no divorce ever, in any part of the Bible, except for 'Sexual Immorality'". If he had been making this universal statement, he would be contradicting Paul who allowed divorce for abandonment (1 Cor. 7.15 – as we will see in chapter 6).

Imagine my wife was dressing to go out and she was wondering whether to wear a jacket over her dress, so she asked me, "Should I wear the jacket?" and I answered, "I think you should just wear the dress." Then imagine my surprise when she comes downstairs wearing the dress and nothing else – no shoes, no stockings or anything – explaining, "Well, you said I should 'just wear the dress'. This is exactly what some people do to Jesus' reply, 'nothing except 'Sexual Immorality'" – instead of regarding this as an answer to a specific question about the two grounds for divorce in Deuteronomy 24.1, they regard it as a universal statement about the whole of Scripture.

Jesus gave the Pharisees a straightforward answer about where he stood in their debate, but actually he was not very interested in this subject. He was much more interested in marriage than divorce, so although he gave this answer in Matthew 19.9, he didn't do so until he had spent the intervening verses talking about marriage, and specifically about matters where he disagreed with both Hillelites and Shammaites.

## Jesus' other teaching on marriage and divorce

Jesus was determined to tell his listeners where they had *all* gone wrong with regard to marriage and divorce – so he went back to basics!

Polygamy was allowed by most Jews in the 1st century (except for the sect at Qumran and a few progressive Jews who taught against it) and was widely practised in Palestine – the only place where Roman law allowed it. Jesus told them that monogamy was the Biblical ideal from the beginning. Jesus alluded to Genesis 2.24 when he said, "So they are no longer **two** but one flesh." He deliberately included the word "two" which is not actually found in the Hebrew text although it was often added there when the Old Testament was translated into other languages such as Greek and Aramaic. The fact that Jesus included the word "two" is therefore very significant. He also pointed out that God made them "male and female" – both singular – which reminded them that the perfect marriage in Eden involved only two people.

Jesus continued by stressing that God intended marriage to be lifelong and that marriage break-up was a tragedy. Therefore instead of divorcing an erring partner, he said that you should try to forgive them. Jesus demonstrated how serious it was to break up a marriage by giving a commandment: "What therefore God has joined together, let not man separate" (Mt. 19.6).

The Pharisees thought that they had a clever answer for this because they said that sometimes Moses instructed that you *must* divorce a wife. They believed that divorce was compul-sory if a woman committed adultery, because Deuteronomy 24.1 said that a man should give a divorce certificate to a wife guilty of "sexual immorality". So they argued with Jesus: "Why then did Moses *command* one to give a certificate of divorce?" (Matthew. 19.7). Jesus replied: "Moses *allowed* you to divorce your wives" (Matthew. 19.8) – i.e. he did not command it, but allowed it. It was not *compulsory*, although it was permissible.

## Divorce only for 'hard-heartedness'

Jesus also said that God does not want us to divorce if we can avoid it, even in the case of adultery; he wants us to forgive an erring partner rather than divorce them. "But surely there's a limit to the number of times we have to forgive?" we say – and I'm sure that the Pharisees also said this, or at least they thought it. So Jesus explained further: "Moses allowed divorce for *hard-heartedness.*"

The Pharisees knew immediately what he meant, but we are not so familiar with the Old Testament so we have to work at it a bit. 'Hard-heartedness' means 'stubbornness' and it is a word which was invented by the translators of the Septuagint – the official Jewish translation of the Old Testament into Greek. It occurs frequently in the Septuagint, but does not occur in ordinary Greek except when people were quoting the Old Testament, so Jesus is presumably alluding to an Old Testament text – but which one? This was not a difficult question for the Pharisees, many of whom knew the Old Testament by heart, because "hard-heartedness" occurs in only one place in the context of divorce – where Jeremiah warned Judah that God might divorce them like he divorced Israel:

> Jer. 4.4 (Septuagint): Circumcise yourselves to your Lord, and circumcise your hard-heartedness.

Jeremiah had described Israel as God's wife at the beginning of this section (Jer. 2.1), and had said that she committed adultery with other gods (Jer. 2.20–26) so that God was forced to divorce her (Jer. 3.1–8), as we saw in more detail in chapter 3. Jeremiah warned Judah that she was going the same way as her sister nation Israel (Jer. 3.10–14) and that she was being hard-hearted (i.e. stubborn) in her adultery (Jer. 4.3–4).

Jesus said that marriage was not like this "from the beginning" (Mt. 19.8). In Eden there was no sin to break up marriages, and therefore there was no need for divorce. But when sin came, and marriages started going wrong, Moses "allowed" divorce for broken marriage vows (Mt. 19.8). Jesus thought that people were being too quick to divorce so he reminded them that Moses only meant divorce to occur when there was 'hard-heartedness' – i.e. a stubborn refusal to repent and stop breaking marriage vows. Jesus said elsewhere that we should forgive people if they sin against us and repent:

> Lk. 17.4: If he sins against you seven times in the day, and turns to you seven times, saying, 'I repent,' you must forgive him.

In marriage, too, we should forgive a partner who sins and repents. However many times they break their vows we should forgive them if they repent and want to change their ways. We should only consider divorce if they continually break their vows with hard-heartedness, i.e. if they stubbornly continue without repenting or trying to change. God found himself in this position when Israel constantly and unrepentantly went running after other gods, until eventually God, who hates divorce, had to divorce her for hard-hearted adultery.

## Dropping the bombshell

The disciples were utterly shocked at this teaching about forgiveness and at Jesus' rejection of the 'Any Cause' type of divorce. Suddenly they realised that marriage was much more serious than they had thought, and that they could not get divorced whenever they wished. They said: "If such is the case of a man with his wife, it is better not to marry." (Mt. 19.10).

At this point Jesus showed how profoundly different his teaching was from the rest of Judaism, because he told his disciples that marriage was optional. All Jews regarded marriage as compulsory because of the command in Scripture, "Be fruitful and multiply" (Gen. 1.28). Even the Qumran sect, who tried to avoid women, got married for about five years when they were twenty, in order to fulfil this command. So when Jesus said that some "have made themselves eunuchs for the sake of the kingdom of heaven" (Mt. 19.12) he was disagreeing with every Jew alive, so far as we know.

But the most shocking part of Jesus' teaching, as far as the general public were concerned, was his rejection of the 'Any Cause' divorces. It meant that they could only divorce their wives on specific Biblical grounds – they could not simply decide they didn't like her looks or her cooking any more. Furthermore, Jesus said that they should forgive a partner who repented and, although he did allow divorce, he said that it should be only as a very last resort.

Jesus did not just say that 'Any Cause' divorces were invalid but emphasised their invalidity by saying that people with 'Any Cause' divorces were not really divorced at all. Therefore, if they remarried after this type of divorce, they were actually committing adultery because they were still married to their previous partner.

## Re-reading the Gospel passage

Much of what I have unpacked here is difficult to follow in the Gospels because the Gospel writers could not record everything verbatim and they removed anything which was obvious. Having unpacked it, we should now have a clearer idea of how a 1st-century reader understood this passage when they read or heard it. I will now go through it again (quoting the English Standard Version, which is a very accurate scholarly translation), in order to put all these details together.

The passage starts with some Rabbis, probably Hillelites, who asked him if he accepted the 'Any Cause' divorces as in Deuteronomy 24.1.

> Mt. 19.3: And Pharisees came up to him and tested him by asking, "Is it lawful to divorce one's wife for any cause?"

Jesus wanted to talk about other things which he thought were more important. First, that a man should marry only one wife, as in Eden.

> Mt. 19.4: He answered, "Have you not read that he who created them from the beginning made them male and female, [5] and said, 'Therefore a man shall leave his father and his mother and hold fast to his wife, and they shall become one flesh'? [6] So they are no longer two but one flesh."

Jesus also said that breaking up a marriage was very serious, because God has heard the couple's wedding vows and joined them with a blessing, as he did in Eden.

> Mt. 19.6b: "What therefore God has joined together, let not man separate."

The Rabbis brought Jesus back to their question by saying that a divorce certificate is *commanded* by Scripture in cases of adultery as in Deuteronomy 24.1.

> Mt. 19.7: They said to him, "Why then did Moses command one to give a certificate of divorce and to send her away?"

Jesus said that divorce was never compulsory, and we should not divorce anyone unless they are hard-hearted – i.e. stubbornly unrepentant, like adulterous Judah in Jeremiah 4.4. People are no longer sinless, like they were in Eden.

> Mt. 19.8: He said to them, "Because of your hardness of heart Moses allowed you to divorce your wives, but from the beginning it was not so."

Coming back to the original question, Jesus said that there was no ground for divorce in Deuteronomy 24.1 except 'Sexual Immorality', so divorces for 'Any Cause' (on which virtually all divorces were based at that time) were   invalid.

> Mt. 19.9: And I say to you: whoever divorces his wife, except for sexual immorality, and marries another, commits adultery."

The disciples were shocked that divorce is so difficult.

Mt. 19.10: The disciples said to him, "If such is the case of a man with his wife, it is better not to marry."

Jesus answered that marriage is not compulsory, and it is not for everyone.

Mt. 19.11–12: But he said to them, "Not everyone can receive this saying, but only those to whom it is given. [12] For there are eunuchs who have been so from birth, and there are eunuchs who have been made eunuchs by men, and there are eunuchs who have made themselves eunuchs for the sake of the kingdom of heaven. Let the one who is able to receive this receive it."

Mark's version is more difficult to understand because it is more highly abbreviated than Matthew's. The main differences are two phrases 'Any Cause' and "nothing except 'Sexual Immorality'" which are found in both of Matthew's accounts (Mt. 19.3–12 and Mt. 5.31–32) but not in those of Mark or Luke (Mk. 10.2–12; Lk. 16.18). Did Mark (and perhaps Luke) remove these well-known phrases because they were not necessary for his readership? Or did Matthew add them in order to help his readers understand the debate? I think both happened. Mark wrote first, and abbreviated the debate as much as possible, but Matthew wrote later, when the debate was more or less over and was less well-known. He knew his readers might get confused, so he helped them out by putting a few details back in.

## Summarising Jesus' teaching

A summary for a modern generation of Jesus' teaching during this debate would be something like:

All divorces based on 'Any Cause' (i.e. groundless divorces) are invalid, because the phrase 'a cause of sexual immorality' (Deut. 24.1) means nothing except 'Sexual Immorality'. Moses never *commanded* divorce but *allowed* us to divorce a partner who is hard-hearted (i.e. who unrepentantly breaks marriage vows, as in Jer. 3–4).

Matthew and Luke both summarised this debate on divorce into one sentence and had to decide which aspects of Jesus' teaching to emphasise: his teaching on monogamy, on marriage not being compulsory, on divorce not being compulsory for adultery, on his opposition to 'Any Cause' divorces, or his plea that we avoid divorce unless the erring partner was sinning 'hard-heartedly'?

Both Matthew and Luke picked the element which was most shocking for ordinary Jews: Jesus' rejection of the 'Any Cause' type of divorce. This affected any family with a divorced person in it – which probably included most families in the land. It only affected those divorces which were based on 'Any Cause', but since this type of divorce had already almost totally replaced the other types of divorce, they could say, for the sake of abbreviation, that Jesus was talking about "everyone who divorces". Jesus had expressed this part of his teaching in a shocking and memorable way (saying that remarriage after this type of divorce was technically adultery), and they retained this in their summarised versions:

> Lk. 16.18: Everyone who divorces his wife and marries another commits adultery, and he who marries a woman divorced from her husband commits adultery.

> Mt. 5.32: But I say to you that everyone who divorces his wife, except on the ground of sexual immorality, makes her commit adultery. And whoever marries a divorced woman commits adultery.

These two texts look at the issue from several different viewpoints, but they come to the same conclusion. They both say that any remarriage would be adulterous because their divorces are invalid and so they are still married to their former partners. The point is that Jesus was so intractably against the 'Any Cause' divorces that he said they were completely invalid.

## To conclude: Questions which Jesus does not answer

What should divorcees do if they have already remarried – should they get divorced from their new partner and remarry their former spouse? Jesus does not tell them, or, if he did, the Gospels do not record it. Fortunately for us, Paul does cover this type of problem as we shall see in chapter 10.

We would also like to know what Jesus thought about other Biblical grounds for divorce. We know that he rejected the new non-Biblical 'Any Cause' divorces and that he accepted divorce for adultery, as in Deuteronomy 24.1, but we do not know what he thought about the three grounds for divorce in Exodus 21.10–11 because no-one asked him about this text – or if they did, the Gospel writers did not think his teaching on this was significant enough to include in their short account. I would guess that for these grounds, like adultery, he would counsel forgiveness rather than divorce, unless they were sinning hard-heartedly, but again, we have to look to Paul in chapters 6 and 8 to fill in this gap in our knowledge.

We might also ask, "How did the church misunderstand Jesus' teaching for so long? How come no-one remembered about 'Any Cause' divorces?" We will look at this in chapter 12.

We found in this chapter that Jesus laid the foundations for a new approach to divorce. He did not replace the Old Testament, or rewrite it, but he emphasised its principles and compassion, saying that the injured partner should forgive the partner who breaks their marriage vows and then repents and that you should only divorce a partner who sins in a hard-hearted way, i.e. one who breaks their vows stubbornly and unrepentantly.

## Further Reading

### *On Jewish customs and Rabbinic debates*

Chapter 5 "Rabbinic teaching" in my *Divorce and Remarriage in the Bible* (Eerdmans, 2002) summarises the evidence from ancient Jewish sources.

The article "Divorce" by D.W. Amram in the *Jewish Encyclopedia* (12 vols, Funk & Wagnalls Co, 1905), vol. 4 624–628, gives a more traditional Jewish view of their literature. The later Rabbis in the Talmud misunderstood Shammai's position (see chapter 7) and this article reflects that misunderstanding.

The Dead Sea sect's teaching has been re-evaluated recently, but one of the best books on the subject is still *Marriage and Ministry in the New Temple. A Study with Special Reference to Matthew 19.13[sic]–12 and 1 Corinthians 11.3–16* by Abel Isaksson, (Gleerup, 1965), who was the first person to show that the Qumran sect did marry like all other Jews, but then they divorced their wives after they had fulfilled the command to have children.

### On the interpretation of the Gospel texts

Chapter 6 "Jesus' teaching" in my *Divorce and Remarriage in the Bible* (Eerdmans, 2002) goes through the Gospel texts in much more detail.

One of the best commentaries on Matthew is Don Carson's in the *Expositor's Bible Commentary* (Zondervan, 1984).

For obscure scholarly details, you can't beat Dale Allison Jn.'s commentary on Matthew in *The International Critical Commentary* (3 vols, T. & T. Clark, 1988–1997).

### On Jesus' teaching against polygamy

For academic details see my article "Jesus' Old Testament basis for Monogamy" in *The Old Testament in the New Testament: Essays in Honour of J.L. North,* ed. Steve Moyise (JNTS Supp. 189, Sheffield Academic Press, 2000).

**6**

# When Your Partner Walks Out

**Christians shouldn't cause divorce but sometimes they have to accept it**

Most of Paul's teaching on marriage and divorce is found in his first letter to the Corinthian church in about AD 55. Corinth was a major cosmopolitan city and was largely made up of Gentiles though there were also a lot of Jews in the city and in the young church. They were having problems applying Jesus' teaching in a city which followed the Roman legal system. To complicate things further, Corinth was in the grip of a terrible famine which made any kind of family life difficult.

## Paul did not disapprove of marriage

It is almost certain that Paul was married when he was younger, though we know that he was single when he wrote 1 Corinthians. Marriage was compulsory for a pious Jew, and Paul said that before his conversion, he was a very religious Pharisee (Acts 23.6; Phil. 3.5). Every Jewish male was expected to marry in order to fulfil God's command to "multiply and fill the earth" (Gen. 1.28) and it was unthinkable that a pious young man would remain single. Paul's wife had probably died in childbirth (as happened all too often in the 1st century) and we can conclude that he knew about marriage personally – its joys, responsibilities and sadnesses.

As well as being compulsory for Jews, marriage was also compulsory in Roman law, though it was rarely enforced. This law was enacted by the emperor Augustus who saw that most Roman young men avoided marriage and fatherhood so that they could enjoy an endless series of affairs. He was worried by the lack of legal sons born into Roman households, and the weakening of the family unit, so in 18 BC he introduced laws which made it compulsory to get married.

Paul contradicted both the Jewish and the Roman laws by teaching in 1 Corinthians 7 that marriage was optional. Corinth, being a Roman city, followed Roman law and many members of its church were former Jews, so they also knew about Jewish law. Paul therefore had a tough job to convince them that if they were not already married, they should not get married – at least, not yet.

Many people think this teaching means that Paul was against marriage, but he was only telling the Corinthians to wait until "the present distress" (v. 26) was over. He did not need to tell them what kind of 'distress' this was, because their suffering was all too obvious to them. Historians guess that he must have been referring to the famine which was afflicting the region at that time. In the 1st century, getting married meant having children, and it is not easy caring for babies and toddlers in a time of famine.

## A question about sex

In general, Paul approved of marriage but there were some Christians in Corinth who *were* against marriage, and who wrote to Paul to ask him if he agreed. Paul quoted a phrase from their letter which encapsulated their viewpoint:

> 1 Cor. 7.1: Now concerning the matters about which you wrote: "It is good for a man not to have sexual relations with a woman."

One translation unfortunately says, "Now for the matters you wrote about: It is good for a man not to marry", so that it looks as if Paul was making this statement himself and that he was against marriage. They were actually the words of some Corinthians who wanted to avoid sex. They thought that they could live holier lives if they avoided women, and one woman had evidently already left her husband (vv. 10–11).

Paul replied by reminding them what their marriage vows were. They had promised to feed, clothe and share conjugal love with their wives, and Paul emphasised that if they neglected conjugal love they would "deprive" their partners.

> 1 Cor. 7.3–4: The husband should give to his wife her conjugal rights, and likewise the wife to her husband. [4] For the wife does not have

authority over her own body, but the husband does. Likewise the husband does not have authority over his own body, but the wife does. [5] Do not deprive one another.

Notice that Paul does not say that either partner can *demand* sexual love because both should regard the other person as ruling over their body. Love is not a matter of taking, but *giving*. Paul is almost using the language of slavery, saying that they should both consider themselves to belong to the other. He has probably been influenced here by the context of the verse on which the marriage vows were based – the law about the rights of the slave wife in Exodus 21.10–11. Also, Paul does not define what this love consists of – because in some situations a cuddle is a warmer expression of conjugal love than intercourse. Paul says that each should be concerned for the needs and wishes of their partner and not for themselves.

The couple could, of course, take a break from sexual relations and Paul recognised that this was sometimes a good thing if it made extra time for prayer. But he also warned them that this should not be done for long, in case their abstinence led to sin.

> 1 Cor. 7.5: Do not deprive one another, except perhaps by agreement for a limited time, that you may devote yourselves to prayer; but then come together again, so that Satan may not tempt you because of your lack of self-control.

This was very similar to the type of rules which the Rabbis made about conjugal rights. The Rabbis also allowed such breaks and defined exactly how long they could be. For instance, you were allowed a longer break if your work took you away from home, and an even longer break if you were a Rabbi, though you got no break at all if you were unemployed. Paul did not make legalistic definitions like these, but just said that they could take a short break for prayer.

## Caring for each other

Paul reminded the Corinthians about their marriage vows by using language and ideas which would have been familiar to them from their Jewish background. Non-Jews would have found these concepts familiar as well because Greek marriage contracts of the time also speak about providing food and clothing, though most of them avoided mentioning conjugal love.

With regard to the vows to feed and clothe each other Paul sum-marised these obligations in a single category which we might call 'material support'. Similarly, the Rabbis had different regulations con-cerning the neglect of physical affection and of material support. They also defined exactly how much the man had to spend on food and cloth and how much cooking and sewing the woman had to do. Paul did not specify quantities and simply said that they had to "please" each other.

> 1 Cor. 7.32–34: I want you to be free from anxieties. The unmarried man is anxious about the things of the Lord, how to please the Lord. [33] But the married man is anxious about worldly things, how to please his wife, [34] and his interests are divided. And the unmarried or betrothed woman is anxious about the things of the Lord, how to be holy in body and spirit. But the married woman is anxious about worldly things, how to please her husband.

Paul sounds rather negative about marriage here but as we said before this was probably due to the famine. It was a difficult time to be mar-ried because it was difficult to keep the vows to provide food and clothes and general material care for each other and Scripture said that if a husband or wife wilfully failed to provide food and clothing, they were guilty of neglect. Although Scripture did not specifically mention abuse, this was implied in the law against neglect. If a husband was not allowed to starve his wife or refuse her money for clothes, then he certainly could not beat his wife or rape or imprison her. Similarly if a wife could not refuse to cook or sow for her husband, she certainly could not beat or poison or torture him.

## Roman divorce was too easy

If anyone *did* do any of these things, there was an easy remedy: their partner could divorce them immediately and without any difficulty using the Roman divorce-by-separation. This was possible because Corinth was run under Roman law and even Jews could choose to use a Roman divorce if they wished. This Roman divorce was very easy – all you had to do was walk out of the house if your partner owned it, or tell your partner to get packing and leave the house if you owned it. There was no need to cite any grounds for ending the marriage and, having separated, you were both legally divorced and free to remarry.

For a victim of an abusive marriage, it was good that under Roman law they could get away from their partner without too much difficulty since they did not have to prove the abuse in court. But the problem was that divorce in Corinth was *too* easy because you did not need any good reason to get divorced, or, in fact, any reason at all. This meant you could walk out on an innocent and loving partner or you could even throw them out of the house if you owned it. Either partner could decide at any time to end the marriage and the other partner became a helpless victim of this whim.

Even Christians in Corinth were using the Roman method of divorce-by-separation. Having separated from their partners they considered themselves divorced and free to remarry which, in Roman law, they *were*. Paul had to remind them about the law of the Old Testament, pointing out that Biblical divorce was always based on the grounds of broken vows, unlike the Roman groundless divorce. Therefore Christians should not practise the Roman divorce-by-separation, i.e. they should not simply separate from their partner and consider themselves legally divorced.

> 1 Cor. 7.10: To the married I give this charge (not I, but the Lord): the wife should not separate from her husband [11] (but if she does, she should remain unmarried or else be reconciled to her husband), and the husband should not dismiss his wife.[13]

## Translating 'separate'

These verses are translated in various ways in different Bibles but it is important to translate them as literally as possible, especially concerning the way in which the separation occurs. Paul describes both the husband and the wife deciding for themselves to divorce. She "separates herself" (i.e. she walks out on him) and he decides to "dismiss his wife" (i.e. send her packing). The differences are in the fact that the husband was the one most likely to own the house, so for the wife to divorce her husband she would have to leave the house (i.e. "separate herself") and for the man to divorce his wife he would have to tell her to leave his house (i.e. "dismiss her"). In this situation Paul was not talking to partners who were divorced against their will since both the man and the woman in these verses made their own decision to separate from their partners.

If you want the technical details of the translation, here they are, but you can ignore them if you prefer:

Paul uses "separate" in the reflexive mood, i.e. "separate themselves", but this Greek form is exactly like the passive mood, i.e. "be separated". This has confused a lot of translators, but in v. 15 Paul used the same word again, with exactly the same form, in a context where it cannot possibly be passive, and must be reflexive: "If the unbelieving partner separates, let it be so." In effect he is saying, if an unbeliever leaves a believer, let them do so because, after all, there is very little the believer can do about it. Now, if "separate" is translated in v. 15 with the passive rather than the reflexive it would be: "If the unbeliever partner is separated, let it be so" – in other words, any believer can leave an unbelieving and, if they do, we should do nothing about it and just let it happen. This is patently the wrong translation because it is exactly the opposite of what Paul had already said in vv. 10–11. Therefore the correct translation is 'separate themselves'.

To leave the technicalities behind, Paul's point is that Christians should not use this Roman form of divorce-by- separation because it was groundless, so it was too easy to divorce someone against their will when they had done nothing wrong. Anybody could just take it on themselves to separate and, by doing so, their partner could suddenly find that they had been legally divorced whether they wanted it or not. For Christians, this was simply not an option.

## What if you have used divorce-by-separation?

But some Christians had *already* used divorced-by-separation and Paul was keen to tell them what to do in that situation.

> 1 Cor. 7.11: If she does [separate herself], she should remain unmarried or else be reconciled to her husband.

He is saying that if someone had separated they should not consider themselves to be divorced but should try to reverse the separation by remaining unmarried while trying to be reconciled again. In other words, they should do all that they can to reverse the Roman divorce-by-separation.

Paul was probably thinking of a particular woman at this point because he says "she", but in the rest of this chapter he is always careful to address both men and women, even to the point of repeating himself in an almost tiresome way. The Corinthians presumably knew which woman Paul was referring to but we can only guess the reason why she separated from her husband. The only clue we have is in v. 1 where Paul quoted the Corinthians' letter to him, where they asked him about the teaching of some groups who thought that holiness included avoiding sex: "It is good for a man not to have sexual relations with a woman" (and vice versa). The woman was probably influenced by one such group but, as we saw above, Paul certainly did not regard this as a Biblical reason for divorce.

Paul pointed out that Jesus himself condemned this type of groundless divorce because he rejected the Jewish groundless divorce (the 'Any Cause' divorce). The only difference in the Roman groundless divorce was that women, as well as men, could initiate it, and Paul assumed that if Jesus condemned the Jewish groundless divorce, then he would condemn the Roman one. This is why Paul tells the Christians that the Lord commands it (v. 10).

## What if you are a victim of divorce-by-separation?

What about the *victim* of a divorce-by-separation? Paul told the person who enacted the separation that they should remain unmarried and try to effect a reconciliation, but what if you have been forced into a divorce by your partner, even though you did not want to split up? Paul addressed this situation in v. 15:

> 1 Cor. 7.15: But if the unbelieving partner separates, let it be so. In such cases the brother or sister is not enslaved. God has called you to peace.[14]

In effect, he said that if a non-Christian divorces you, you should let them go. This seems like a sudden u-turn – as if Paul does not care and as though he does not want marriages between Christians and non-Christians to continue. But we know this is *not* true because he said the opposite in vv. 12–14 where he told Christians not to divorce their non-Christian partner:

> 1 Cor. 7.12–13: If any brother has a wife who is an unbeliever, and she consents to live with him, he should not dismiss her. [13] If any woman has a husband who is an unbeliever, and he consents to live with her, she should not dismiss him.[15]

So Paul does not want Christians to divorce their non-Christian partners and yet he says that Christians should let non-Christians divorce them. This does not seem to make sense until we look at it pragmatically. Ask yourself, what can the divorced Christian partner do? Their non-Christian husband or wife has told them the marriage is over; the husband has dismissed his wife or the wife has walked out. What can Paul tell the Christian to do to reverse this divorce? Of course, they should have been doing their utmost to hold the marriage together before the divorce, but once it has happened, any attempts at reconciliation are unlikely to work and are likely to be seen as pestering.

Paul taught that once such a divorce has happened, a line should be drawn under it, saying, in effect, "If they divorce you, there is not much you can do; if the actual divorce-by-separation has happened, then let them go." He then added that God has called us to peace, and not to endless conflict after the divorce.

## To conclude: Divorce should be the last option

Paul and Jesus have the same message for two different cultures:

1. Believers should never cause a divorce – i.e. they should not break their marriage vows.
2. Believers should not use a groundless divorce – i.e. Jews should not use the new Hillelite 'Any Cause' divorce, and no-one should use the Roman "divorce-by-separation".

Jesus added that believers should do all they can to save a marriage, which includes forgiving a partner who breaks vows and then repents. And Paul added that believers who have wrongly enacted a divorce-by-separation should attempt to be reconciled and not remarry because this would make the divorce irreversible.

Paul said further that if someone is divorced against their will, they may accept it. There is nothing they can do to reverse the divorce, and God has called them to peace.

But this leaves us with two questions:

• Can a believer divorce a partner who breaks their vows unrepentantly?
• And can a believer remarry after a divorce?

These questions will be answered in following chapters, but first we have to ask a more fundamental question: Do marriages *ever* end in the sight of God?

## Further Reading

*On Roman divorce law*

A couple of good introductions to Roman divorce law:
"Divorce of Jews in the Roman Empire" by Alfredo M. Rabello (*The Jewish Law Annual*, ed. B.S. Jackson, E.J. Brill, 1981, 4:79–102).

"Divorce Roman Style: How easy and how frequent was it?" by Susan Treggiari (ch. 2 in Beryl Rawson, ed. *Marriage, Divorce and Children in Ancient Rome*, Clarendon Press, 1991, 31–46).

*On Graeco-Roman divorce vocabulary*

I have analysed the Graeco-Roman legal texts from the 1st century in "1 Corinthians 7 in the light of the Graeco-Roman Marriage and Divorce Papyri" (*Tyndale Bulletin* 52, 2001, 101–116).

This was based on the collection of all the divorce and marriage documents in Greek and Latin from the 1st century and surrounding centuries which I have published on the Web as:

*Marriage and Divorce Papyri of the Ancient Greek, Roman and Jewish World* (Web publication, 2000) http://www.Tyndale.cam.ac.uk/Brewer/MarriagePapyri.

*On interpreting 1 Corinthians 7*

Chapter 7 "Paul's Teaching" in my *Divorce and Remarriage in the Bible* (Eerdmans, 2002) deals with this chapter in much more detail.

The best commentary is Gordon Fee's *The First Epistle to the Corinthians* (The New International Commentary on the New Testament, Eerdmans, 1987).

# Till Death Us Do Part?

**Is a divorcee still married in God's eyes?**

What is in the middle of both America and Australia? Answer: The letter "R".

Another riddle: If a woman is born in Italy, marries in England, moves to America, and dies in Baltimore, what is she?

I must admit that when I first heard this I did not get it at all. Several possibilities came to mind: What is the first letter of each place? I E A B. Or what shape did her journey make? Or what is at the first letter of the place where she was born, and the last letter of the place where she died? But I was on completely the wrong track because I ignored the obvious – a woman born in Italy, married in England, moved to America and died in Baltimore, what is she? Answer: Dead!

Alright, here is another seemingly simple riddle with a catch: A woman falls in love, gets engaged, and gets married. Her husband commits adultery, moves in with his mistress and divorces her. What is her marital status? The obvious answer is: "Single" or "Divorced". But many Bible scholars would say: "Married – because only death can end a marriage."

## Lifelong marriage can be a curse

*Is* death the only end to marriage? If it was, some people would regard this as a blessing from God because it represents a lifetime guarantee on their marriage. But others, who have found that the person they married is actually unfaithful or violent, would see it as a life sentence of imprisonment with a most cruel enemy.

Few things last for ever, or even for a lifetime, and this is what makes marriage such a special event in someone's life. Someone has proposed to you, saying, "I love you and only you," and at the wedding they say: "I will love you, honour you and keep you through poverty and illness, till death us do part." Is there anything more affirming than someone you love making this lifelong commitment to you? That is why it is so devastating when those vows are broken. But it happens.

People commit adultery, or become cruel or abusive and their marriage starts to break down. What happens then? Most marriages can be healed, with effort from both partners, but, like cancer if it is left untreated too long, broken vows are terminal because they kill a marriage.

When a marriage has reached this condition, a Christian can do one of three things:

1. Remain together and suffer, in the hope that things will get better.
2. Separate, but without getting divorced.
3. Get divorced.

But should a Christian ever get divorced? Doesn't marriage last forever?

Some Christians say "once married, always married". I would love to say that this is true, and that all marriages can be saved; that God blesses each marriage and keeps it together whatever happens, but I have some bad news for you. Some marriages cannot be rescued, and the Bible does not promise that all marriages have a lifetime guarantee.

## Texts which might imply lifelong marriage

It's true that a few texts in the Bible do seem to say that only death can end a marriage, but this is only when the context or the actual words used are ignored. One example of this is the saying, "Those whom God has joined, no-one can separate." As we saw in the first chapter, what the text actually says is "*let* no-one separate" – which implies that marriage *can* end, though this is very undesirable.

There are three other texts in the New Testament which appear to say that all marriages last for a lifetime, and two which seem to say that only death can end a marriage. The rest of this chapter is going to examine these texts in their context. You may be tempted to skip this chapter, but please don't, because it is central for understanding the Biblical basis of remarriage.

The first text is when Jesus described remarriage after divorce as "adultery" (Mt. 19.9 and parallels), which implies that a divorced person is still married. However, as we saw in chapter 5, Jesus was specifically referring to the new 'Any Cause' divorces rather than all types of divorce. He condemned the 'Any Cause' divorces as un-Biblical and invalid – and said that if you get remarried after an invalid divorce, you are technically committing adultery. So rather than Jesus saying in this text that marriage lasts a lifetime, in context he is simply emphasising that the 'Any Cause' divorce was not a valid one.

The second way in which Scripture appears to support the "marriage lasts a lifetime" teaching is when it describes a married couple as "one flesh", which seems to imply a permanent condition that can only end with death (Mt. 19.5–6 and parallels). It sounds like two people have permanently become a new individual. This is, of course, what *should* happen and it is sad that it's not always how things turn out.

Paul points out that people sadly can become 'one flesh' with prostitutes (1 Cor. 6.15–20) and says that this is a very serious sin because Christians are a Temple of the Holy Spirit. But he did not say that a 'one flesh' relationship with a prostitute was permanent. If it was, he would have had to warn those at Corinth who were converted fornicators (1 Cor. 6.11) that they must remain single because their previous 'one flesh' relationship prohibited them from getting married. Paul certainly regarded a one-flesh relationship as more intimate than any other, but he did not think that it was, by definition, a permanent relationship. So although it describes a relationship which *should* be lifelong, this phrase does not guarantee that it *will* last for a lifetime.

The last text which appears to imply that marriage is always lifelong is Ephesians 5.32. In the original Greek, Christ's marriage to the church is described as a "mystery" (Greek *mustérion*) but when the Greek was translated into Latin the word *mustérion* or mystery was translated as "sacrament" (Latin *sacramentum*). This was a perfectly good translation in the 4th century because *sacramentum* meant 'a secret, hidden in holiness', but over subsequent centuries the meaning of 'sacrament' started to change. By medieval times the word 'sacrament' had come to mean 'an unchangeable sacred reality', such as the Sacrament of the Priesthood which refers to a permanent transformation of a lay person into a priest when he makes his vows before the bishop. Similarly, the Sacrament of Marriage refers to the permanent transformation of two individuals into a married couple when they make their vows before a priest.

Whether or not you agree with the theology of sacraments, there is no Biblical basis for saying that marriage is a sacrament, except for the

Latin Vulgate translation of Ephesians 5.32 which was made when 'sacrament' meant something similar to 'mystery'.

These suggestions that marriage is always lifelong turn out to have no Biblical foundation but there are still two important texts we must examine which both appear to say that only death can end a marriage. These two texts (in 1 Cor. 7 and Rom. 7) are actually more important for what they do *not* say, because although they both say that death can end a marriage, neither of them mentions divorce. This type of reasoning is called 'an argument from silence.' Before we examine these texts we have to know how to decide when an argument from silence is relevant and when the silence is merely coincidental.

## When silence speaks volumes

An argument from silence depends on the assumption that the silence is very significant, but how can you tell if the silence is deliberate or incidental? Sometimes a silence is the key to understanding a passage but at other times it is no more significant than neglecting to say, "I love you" at the end of a phone call – and drawing conclusions from this type of silence can lead to huge misunderstandings!

Jesus used silence in a very significant way with the Rich Young Ruler (Mt. 19.16–22; Lk. 18.18–23). The first four of the Ten Commandments deal with God and the last six deal with man, and when Jesus asked the young man if he kept the commandments, Jesus listed the second section – he was interested in how this ruler interacted with humanity. Actually Jesus only listed commandments 5–9 and then fell silent, missing out number 10. The Rich Young Ruler ignored the silence and said he'd obeyed them all, but of course Jesus had been *deliberately* silent about that last commandment which is "You shall not covet" – i.e. do not long for what others own. Jesus knew that this was where the young man's difficulty lay, and he proved it by asking him to do something which he never asked of anyone else: Give away all your wealth. Jesus knew the rich young ruler couldn't do it because his besetting sin was covetousness, and instead of asking for help with that sin, the man went away sad.

But there are other times when it is very difficult to know if the silence is significant. Have you noticed that the New Testament never talks about musical instruments in the church? Old Testament believers used all kinds of instruments to worship God, especially in the Psalms, but in the New Testament instruments are only mentioned in non-Christian worship or in heaven. Ephesians says that Christians worship with "psalms and hymns and spiritual songs" (Eph. 5.19), but not with instruments. Because of this omission, many Christian groups used to reject all instruments, so their worship was led with voices only, in order to be faithful to Scripture. The introduction of the organ and other musical instruments is a relatively modern innovation which several Christian leaders resisted because of this silence about musical instruments, and one denomination still follows this tradition.

There is one silence in Scripture which inspired the start of a whole new sect. Right at the start of Genesis in the story of the creation of Eve it says that God put Adam to sleep, but it does not say anywhere that God woke him up. If this silence is significant it implies that Adam is still asleep now, so everything which has happened since then is all part of Adam's dream! Mary Baker Eddy noticed this and founded the Christian Scientists. She said that since we are living in Adam's dream, our illnesses are merely illusions and as soon as we realise the truth, those illnesses and other problems will evaporate.

How can we tell if a silence in Scripture is significant or not? The best way is to ask ourselves: Is the silence surprising? Would the original reader or hearer say to themselves: "How strange – he missed that out"? When Jesus missed out one of the Ten Commandments it was obvious and startling but when the New Testament neglects to mention Jesus ever going to the bathroom it is just that there were more important things to say.[16] It is no more significant than the fact that all the references to toilets are in the Old Testament. Perhaps a new denomination will arise which will refuse to build toilets on church property!

## Romans 7.2: The church as Christ's bride

Now we come to the silence about divorce in these two texts, and we have to ask in both cases whether the silence is surprising and significant – i.e. does the absence of divorce in these texts imply that marriage cannot end through divorce? We will find that the silence is not at all unexpected in these texts because the context rules out any mention of ending a marriage through divorce.

The first text is Romans 7.2, although we have to read it in the context of vv. 1–4

Rom. 7.1–4: Do you not know, brothers – for I am speaking to those who know the law – that the Law is binding on a person only as long as he lives? [2] Thus a married woman is bound by law to her husband while he lives, but if her husband dies she is released from the law of marriage. [3] Accordingly, she will be called an adulteress if she lives with another man while her husband is alive. But if her husband dies, she is free from that law, and if she marries another man she is not an adulteress. [4] Likewise, my brothers, you also have died to the Law through the body of Christ, so that you may belong to another, to him who has been raised from the dead, in order that we may bear fruit for God.

This can be summarised as:

"People are tied to the Law of Moses till they die, just as a wife is tied to her husband till death. If she went with another man this would be adultery, unless her husband had died. Therefore God lets you die with Christ, in order to set you free to marry Christ."

Paul compared our relationship to the law to that of a woman's relationship to her husband. A Jewish believer is like someone who is married to the law – a demanding perfectionist who can never be pleased. This believer meets Christ and falls in love with him, but she cannot marry him because if she did she would be committing adultery. All she can do is wait until the marriage ends through death – although, of course, her husband, the law, is eternal and so her wait is hopeless. But the wonderful news which Paul brings is that Christ died for her, and she has died with Christ, therefore her marriage to the law *has* ended through death – her death – and now she is free to marry Christ!

This is a wonderful picture of Christ's love, whose death frees us from the law. The passage tells us a great deal about our salvation, but we should not expect it to teach us about divorce and remarriage. Just as the parable of the sower is not a good manual for learning about farming, so we should not expect to learn much about marriage from an illustration about a believer's marriage to the law and to Christ.

Nevertheless, the woman in this picture thinks her marriage can only end through death, so this might seem to imply that it cannot end through divorce or through desertion. But how *could* her marriage to the law end in these ways? The law would never desert her or break his marriage vows in any way that would lead to divorce because, being the law, he would always keep them *to the letter*! So the whole concept of divorce or desertion is out of place in this picture and no reader would expect Paul to mention them or be surprised at their absence. In fact it would be astonishing if divorce or desertion *were* mentioned, because they would make the illustration break down.

## 1 Corinthians 7.39: widows' freedom to remarry

The other text which fails to mention divorce is 1 Corinthians 7.39. The first half of chapter 7 is addressed to those who are married (vv. 1–17) and in the second half (vv. 25–40) Paul talks to various types of unmarried people, including virgins, those 'released' from marriage and those promised in marriage, till finally, in v. 39, those who are widowed.

> 1 Cor. 7.39: A wife is bound to her husband as long as he lives. But if her husband dies, she is free to be married to whom she wishes, only in the Lord.

Since he is addressing people whose marriages have ended because of the death of their partner, we should not be surprised that Paul does not mention divorce, which would be completely out of place in this context. Here too, it is wrong to think that the text implies that marriage always lasts until death, because the reason for the silence about divorce is simply that it would not have been mentioned in this context.

The reason Paul said this to the widows was in order to free them from the Old Testament law of Levirate marriage (Deut. 25.5–10), which many Jews still imposed on widows. According to this law, a widow without a son had to marry her brother-in-law to ensure there was a male to inherit the family land in Israel. However, by the 1st century, most families had long ago sold their land or lost it permanently, or lived outside the Land of Israel, so the Levirate law no longer made sense and many Jewish leaders were beginning to ignore it. They saw that it had become nothing more than an unnecessary burden on widows who felt forced into a loveless marriage with their brother-in-law. Paul was the first Jew (as far as we know) to say explicitly that this law should no longer apply. He told all widows: You may marry whoever you like – i.e. you do not have to marry your brother-in-law if you do not want to.

## To conclude: Case not proved

We have come to the end of this chapter having learnt what seems to be a very negative message. We have failed to find any evidence that God gives a lifetime guarantee with every marriage. Although some people might be disappointed by this, there will be others – those who are suffering cruel abuse or who have been deserted – who may be relieved to hear that God does not imprison them in a marriage when their partner has so obviously and painfully broken it up.

We have learnt that God is not constrained by any supposed universal law that marriage lasts a lifetime, and we have found nothing in the Bible which speaks about any such rule. Instead, we find that:

- Jesus commands those who have been joined through marriage vows that they should never separate, but the sinner who disregards Jesus' command *can* still break up the marriage.

- The phrase 'one flesh' describes a very real unity which married partners find together in sexual union, but it is not necessarily permanent – especially when that union is with a prostitute.
- Although marriage is as special as any sacrament, this does not guarantee that it will last forever – marriages *don't* always last until death.

- Just because divorce is absent from two texts it does not mean that this silence is significant, especially when divorce would not fit into the context – as is the case with the two texts which are usually cited.

We have found no reason to believe that God changed his mind about divorce between the Old Testament and the New Testament. In both Testaments God is on the side of the victim of marriage break-up, and allows the victim to divorce a partner who is unfaithful or neglectful or abusive.

We do also have a positive conclusion – that God understands us. He lovingly provides a way out of an impossible situation rather than inflexibly and legalistically ruling that all marriages must continue until death, regardless of how faithless or abusive your partner is to you. God abhors the sin of broken marriage vows but he knows our limitations and wants to deal with our sinfulness. He sees what people suffer in secret and gives comfort and a practical solution to the victim. Divorce does not take away the hurt, but it does not perpetuate it either. Even if the victim of a marriage break-up cannot find love elsewhere, they can at least find peace and they can feel safe in the knowledge that the one who betrayed their love no longer has any claim on their life.

These conclusions leave us asking a question: If divorce is possible, *when* is it possible? We will look at this in the next chapter.

## Further Reading

### Bible teaching about lifelong marriage

The best account which disagrees with mine is *Divorce and Remarriage: Biblical Principles and Pastoral Practice* by Andrew Cornes (Hodder & Stoughton, 1993).

A good historical overview of how this doctrine arose is found in *To Have and To Hold: The Marriage Covenant and the Discipline of Divorce* by David Atkinson (Collins, 1979).

### On interpreting the 'difficult' texts

An extremely detailed analysis of Romans 7.2 is found in "Paul's use of analogy: A structural Analysis of Romans 7.1–6" by Joyce A. Little (*Catholic Biblical Quarterly* 46, 1984, 82–90).

Erasmus was the first person to interpret these texts in the light of their context, and other Reformers followed him. This history is dealt with well in *The New Testament Logia on Divorce – a study of their Interpretation from Erasmus to Milton* by V. Norskov Olsen (Mohr-Siebeck, 1971).

# 8

# Four Biblical Grounds for Divorce

### Including abuse and neglect

Someone emailed me with the following story:

> I was the adult Sunday School teacher in a Baptist church and my
> pastor invited me to sit with the deacons and himself in a difficult
> decision. A young lady had been constantly threatened by her alco-
> holic husband. One afternoon, he came to her with a shotgun while
> she was visiting her sister. After chasing her out into a field, he
> pinned her down, put the shotgun to her head and pulled the trig-
> ger, but the gun jammed. He served a few months in the county jail.
> My pastor explained that our church took a hard and fast view that
> divorce was always sin, so if we followed that we would be advis-
> ing her to reconcile with her husband once he was released from jail.
> As I pondered that, I could not believe that God could possibly ask
> her to do that and I said so. The decision that was eventually made
> was that she could separate from him, but not divorce and was to
> live the rest of her life in that state unless he died. I felt this was bet-
> ter for her than reconciliation, but I didn't have complete peace with
> that either.

Although this is an extreme example, any Christian counsellor will tell
you that abuse within a marriage is very common and a huge number
of people live in fear in their own homes. The husband or wife who is
the victim of physical abuse or emotional torture by their partner live
as if they are imprisoned in a double cell with their worst enemy. As
much as we would like to believe otherwise, it happens within
Christians marriages as well, although it is difficult to tell exactly how
frequently because those involved are often too ashamed or embar-
rassed to admit it even to a friend or relative.

## The church struggles to be just

The church has struggled with its handling of these situations for centuries. Origen, the greatest of the Church Fathers at the start of the third century, faced the issue squarely in his Commentary on Matthew.[17] He asked why Jesus did not allow a husband to divorce a wife who had tried to poison him or who had killed one of their children, because "to endure sins of such heinousness which seem to be worse than adultery or fornication, will appear to be irrational". Even though he did not understand how it could possibly be right or just, Origen concluded that we should nevertheless obey Jesus' teaching because it would be "impious" to do otherwise.

In modern times most Christian teachers would likewise say: "I know it sounds harsh, but unless your believing partner has committed adultery, the New Testament is clear that you must stay with them and trust God who has bound you together." Andrew Cornes, who wrote an excellent book in support of this traditional church teaching (*Divorce and Remarriage: Biblical Principles and Pastoral Practice*), gives one concession – he says that if your life is at risk because of the amount of abuse you are suffering, then you are allowed to *separate*, though you may not divorce. Many others extend this concession to include all abusive marriages. We may well sympathise with this way of solving the problem – it does, after all, seem fairer for a victim of abuse to be allowed to separate even if they cannot divorce – but the solution is not Biblical. A couple should not separate without getting divorced because Paul specifically says that married couples may not separate (1 Cor. 7.10–11). So, if we take the traditional interpretation of the New Testament seriously, no-one may separate from an abusing partner.

We have already seen that God gave clear and fair laws in the Old Testament to limit the damage caused by the sin of neglect and abuse – the victim was allowed to decide whether or not they wanted the marriage to end. Would God really have abandoned this wise and practical approach in New Testament times, or is it a principle for the church today? In this chapter we will find that neither Jesus nor Paul abrogate these Old Testament principles, and that Paul assumes that they are still in force.

## Why was Jesus silent about the victim's right to divorce?

It seems surprising that Jesus should ignore this important, ethical Old Testament principle on divorce, especially when he gave such serious warnings about neglecting even the smallest commandment. The occasion when the Pharisees ask him about their 'Any Cause' divorce would have been a perfect time to say something because, as we saw in chapter 5, Jesus took this opportunity to speak to them about many other aspects of marriage and divorce which they did not ask him about. He took the opportunity to speak about the ideal of life-long marriage, the fact that divorce was never compulsory, and that marriage was not compulsory, as well as teaching them about monogamy and, of course, about his interpretation of "a cause of sexual immorality" – that it meant only "Sexual Immorality" and not also 'Any Cause'.[18] So, if Jesus believed that neglect and abuse were valid grounds for divorce, why didn't he say something about them?

The most likely answer is that he did not need to say anything – or he *did* say something, but the Gospel writers did not think it was necessary to record it – because it was something which was so universally accepted that there was no dispute about it. There are several other universally accepted truths which Jesus did not teach anywhere, such as the doctrine that there is only one God. The oneness of God was agreed by everyone, so there was no need for Jesus to teach it. He was also silent about rape and manslaughter but this does not mean that he was unconcerned about victims of these crimes.

The matters about which Jesus *did* speak out (marriage not being compulsory, divorce not being compulsory after adultery, polygamy not being acceptable and divorce for 'Any Cause') were those where his teaching was *against* the teaching of either all or some 1st-century Jews. There were no debates about the validity of neglect and abuse as grounds for divorce in *any* ancient Jewish literature, for the same reason that there are none about the oneness of God – they were principles that were unanimously agreed on. Rather than indicating that Jesus did not accept the validity of divorce for neglect and abuse, his silence about it highlights the fact that he *did* accept it, like all other Jews at that time.

## Didn't Jesus allow only one ground for divorce?

If it is the case that Jesus did accept other valid grounds, how do we reconcile that with his statement that there was only *one* valid ground for divorce, when he said (in Mt. 19.9 and parallels) there was no divorce "except for 'Sexual Immorality'"?

Although it does initially sound like a contradiction, it is only so if Jesus meant that adultery was the only valid ground for divorce in

*Scripture*, whereas the Gospels imply that he meant adultery was the only valid ground which is found *in Deuteronomy 24.1*. As we saw in chapter 5 the Gospels record the whole debate as if it was concerned solely with divorces in Deuteronomy 24.1.

First the Pharisees opened the debate by asking, "Is it lawful to divorce one's wife for 'Any Cause'?" which was a direct reference to the controversial phrase in Deuteronomy 24.1, "A cause of sexual immorality". Also the Pharisees' question "Is it lawful to divorce *one's wife...?*"[19] implied that they were concerned with divorces which can only be initiated by a man. Since the types of divorce in Exodus 21 could be initiated by both men *and* women, the question demonstrates that they were specifically concerned with the types of divorce in Deuteronomy 24.1 which could only be initiated by a man.

As we saw in chapter 5, Jesus ignored the question at first and spoke instead about marriage – which he considered more important than divorce – but the Pharisees again tried to restrict the debate to Deuteronomy 24.1 by reminding Jesus about the "certificate of divorce". All the Old Testament teaching on this is in Deuteronomy 24.1, and it is not mentioned in Exodus 21 or anywhere else in the Law of Moses. All this shows that the only thing which the Pharisees wanted was a straight answer from Jesus about his interpretation of "a cause of sexual immorality" in Deuteronomy 24.1.

Jesus gave them their answer and it was one which they recognised immediately because it was the same as that of the Shammaite Pharisees who said that there is no valid divorce in Deuteronomy 24.1 "except for 'Sexual Immorality'" – i.e. a divorce for 'Sexual Immorality' is valid but a divorce for 'Any Cause' is not.

When the Shammaites said there was no divorce "except for 'Sexual Immorality'" they did not mean that they rejected the validity of other Biblical grounds for divorce because we have records of debates they had with the Hillelites about these grounds – the neglect of food and clothing. These debates were not about whether or not divorce for neglect was *valid* – that was accepted – but they were about how to *define* neglect. They debated the minimum quantities of food and clothing which had to be provided and the amount of 'conjugal love' that was necessary to avoid being charged with 'neglecting' your partner.

It is somewhat surprising to find out from the Talmud that some Rabbis a century or so later thought that the early Shammaites *did* reject all grounds for divorce in Scripture except for 'Sexual Immorality'. These Rabbis lived about 200 years after the demise of the Shammaite cause, so perhaps their mistake is understandable. By that time all Jews followed Hillelite teaching and they had long forgotten what the Shammaites had actually believed. They quoted the slogan "nothing except sexual immorality" thinking that it meant 'this is the only type of divorce in the whole of *Scripture*'. They forgot that the original context of this Shammaite slogan was the debate about the types of divorce *just in Deuteronomy 24.1*.[20]

Christian interpreters have made exactly the same mistake with the words of Jesus. Like the later Rabbis, they forgot (or did not realise) that the context of the phrase "nothing except 'Sexual Immorality'" was the answer to a question about the meaning of Deuteronomy 24.1. Jesus used exactly the same words as the Shammaites in exactly the same context (a debate about Deut. 24.1) with exactly the same people (the Pharisees) in the same time and place (1st-century Palestine), so we have to conclude that Jesus and the Shammaites meant the same thing – i.e. 'there is only one valid type of divorce *in Deuteronomy 24.1*'. Neither he nor the Shammaites implied by this that 'there is only one valid type of divorce *in the whole of Scripture*'.

We have concluded that Jesus' words in Matthew 19.9 (and parallels) only exclude divorce for 'Any Cause', but does this mean that Jesus accepted the grounds given in Exodus 21.10–11? As we saw earlier in this chapter, we can probably assume that he did accept them because if he had not he would have said so. This law in Exodus is not as self-evident to us as it was to 1st-century Jews so this conclusion is, perhaps, not so obvious to us. Fortunately Paul *does* specifically refer to this law.

## Paul teaches four grounds for divorce

In 1 Corinthians 7 Paul referred to the three grounds for divorce in Exodus 21 when he replied to the Corinthians' question about leaving their partners (see chapter 6).

> Ex. 21.10: If he takes another wife to himself, he shall not diminish her food, her clothing, or her conjugal love.[21]

He reminded those who wanted to stop physical relations with their husband or wife that they had made a vow to share "conjugal love" with them (vv. 3–5) and later in the chapter, when he suggested that people should postpone their marriage plans because of the famine, he reminded them that marriage involved promising to clothe and feed their partner, which he summarised as being "anxious about worldly things, how to please" each other (vv. 32–34).

Paul's readers would immediately have recognised his references to these grounds for divorce, even if they were not Jews, because they had also become the basis for Greek and Roman marriage and divorce law. This law spread throughout the whole known world via the Babylonian and then the Persian empires, through to Greek culture and eventually to Roman law. These three grounds for divorce were written into both Jewish and Graeco-Roman marriage documents. This meant that if you were suffering neglect from your husband or wife you could present your case in any court – Roman, Rabbinic, Egyptian or, as far as we know, *any* of the other provincial legal systems of the 1st-century civilised world.

Therefore, although Paul does not specifically say that these three areas of neglect can be grounds for divorce, the fact that he talks about them as obligations implies that he accepted them and agreed with them. The Scripture text from which they come (Ex. 21.10–11) is primarily concerned with releasing the neglected person from the marriage – i.e. the three obligations are merely a secondary meaning which are inferred from the grounds for divorce in this text. If he did *not* accept these grounds for divorce he would not have used these verses as a basis for his teaching on the obligations within marriage.

As well as these three grounds of divorce for neglect, Paul presumably also allowed divorce on the ground of adultery. Although he does not say so, most interpreters assume that he did allow this because Jesus allowed it. Another reason for believing that he allowed it was because, like these three grounds of neglect, adultery was universally recognised as a ground for divorce. Therefore, as with all the other Biblical grounds for divorce, Paul would have had to state very clearly that he disagreed with it if he did not want believers to assume that he permitted divorces on these grounds.

Paul said virtually nothing about divorce itself, and perhaps he deliberately avoided this subject because he wanted to present a more hopeful teaching. By emphasising the obligations within marriage he was hoping that the need for divorces on these grounds would never arise. Certainly they never *should* arise, if believers obeyed this teaching. He was keen for Christians to avoid causing a marriage break-up and so he stressed the four Biblical *obligations in marriage* rather than the four Biblical grounds for divorce, hoping that the need for divorces would not arise. Certainly they never *should* arise, if believers obeyed this teaching.

However, Paul did not expect that unbelievers would necessarily follow this teaching and, as we saw in chapter 6, he told believers that if they were abandoned by their unbelieving partners, they were "not enslaved" (1 Cor. 7.15). As we will see in the next chapter this phrase is a reference to divorce and so Paul is telling believers that they can regard abandonment as a valid divorce. He does not say why, but it would have been obvious to any 1st-century reader – and is obvious to us now that we understand the principles of Exodus 21.10 – that if they were the victim of desertion, they had the right to divorce on the grounds of neglect.

In summary, Paul accepted all four Old Testament grounds for divorce. He accepted 'unfaithfulness' as a ground because this was allowed by Jesus (Deut. 24.1) and he also accepted 'neglect of food, clothing and conjugal love' in Exodus 21.10–11.

## Defining Biblical grounds for divorce

How can we apply and define these four grounds for divorce in the 21st century?

'Unfaithfulness' is of course easily understood, though it is too easy sometimes to condemn the adultery and ignore the neglect which caused the rift and eventually resulted in adultery. Although neglect by one partner does not excuse adultery by the other, it is important to realise that the fault is usually not just one-sided.

'Provision of food and clothing' is summarised by Paul as 'caring for' or 'pleasing' each other (1 Cor. 7.32, 34). As we saw in chapter 6, Paul does not define the amount of care to be provided (like the Rabbis did), but said that we should aim to please each other, which means that he was more concerned with the motivation for caring than with legalistic details.

'Provision of conjugal love' is the most difficult of the marital obligations to define, especially if someone is using it as a ground for divorce. The Rabbis went to the lengths of defining how many times a man had to make love to his wife, specifying different intervals for different occupations. Most men had to do their duty twice a week, though ass drivers only once a week (because they often went on trips for a few days to deliver goods), and those without work were expec-ted to fulfil their obligation every night. There were no such rules for women, probably because the Rabbis considered them to be rapacious individuals who were always pestering their husbands.

The Rabbis were reluctant to allow a divorce on the ground of refusing conjugal activity and in such situations they tried to resolve the issue by talking to the offender, or by applying gradually increasing fines. Therefore if a woman continuously refused her husband, a Rabbinic court could fine her by reducing her *ketubah* (her marriage inheritance) a little each week, and if a man refused his wife then her *ketubah* could be increased a little each week.

We should also look for the principles which are behind these requirements, because a husband who never lets his wife buy make-up, medical supplies or occasional leisure items such as books or CDs has not, strictly speaking, neglected her food or clothing. Similarly, a man who makes love to his wife once a week but never shows her any other kind of affection could be said to fulfil his obligation to provide 'conjugal love', but it would be very legalistic to say that he was fulfilling her needs. The principle behind 'food and clothing' can be called 'material support' and the principle behind 'conjugal love' can be called 'physical affection'. When neglect becomes positive harm it turns into abuse – neglect of material support becomes physical abuse and neglect of physical affection turns into emotional abuse.

### How can one define 'conjugal love'?

Paul does not define the frequency of conjugal activity or suggest fines for withholding it like the Rabbis did, but he tells both partners that they should regard conjugal love as if it were a debt which they owe to each other (1 Cor. 7.3–5). Paul is careful not to say that anyone has the right to demand conjugal love, but says that both partners owe this support, because love is something which we give and not something which we take.

The term 'conjugal love' should not be defined as narrowly as 'sexual intercourse', because this can become impractical or inappropriate in cases of illness or frailty. Physical affection can be demonstrated in many different ways, and often a hug is far more appreciated than intercourse.

The most difficult question is how broadly we can extend the principle of 'physical affection'. The Hebrew word for 'love' in Exodus 21.10 (*onathah*) is very difficult to define because it occurs so rarely, but the most likely meaning is 'conjugal love', which is how the ancient Rabbis interpreted it. We can accept their interpretation as a good indication of its meaning partly because they had access to ancient traditions about what it meant, but mostly because neither Jesus nor Paul felt that it was necessary to correct any misconceptions which they had on this point. The Rabbis extended this 'love' to include respect, because they allowed a woman to divorce a man who demanded that she did degrading things or someone who refused to let her visit her relatives.[22] Peter may have had this concept of respect or honour in mind when he said: "Likewise, husbands, live with your wives in an understanding way, showing honour" (1 Pet. 3.7).

What about couples who are no longer 'in love' with each other – can they get divorced on the ground that there is a neglect of 'love'? It would be very difficult to say that the modern concept of being 'in love' can be read back into any text in the Bible, though it might be possible for someone to conclude that this was implied in the underlying principle of 'physical affection'. However, when we remember that Jesus emphasised divorce should only occur when there is 'hard-hearted' breaking of vows, this suggests that he would be against a divorce for something like 'falling out of love' which does not involve the breaking of any vows or any actual harm to either partner.

Therefore, although the obligation of providing 'conjugal love' in Exodus 21.10 can be regarded as the foundation of a principle of 'physical affection' or even perhaps 'respect', it should not be spread so broadly that the concept of life-long marriage is weakened. Marriage is based on promises, not just on feelings. When the heat of passion cools, this is not a signal that the marriage is coming to an end, but that the marriage needs attending to. No-one sells their house just because the heating system needs repair!

## So what can we say to the abused?

Now that we are aware that the grounds for divorce in the Bible include the principles of material support and physical affection, what do we say to the woman who has a violent, abusive husband? Firstly, we can tell her that God's law has taken such sin into account. God's ideal for marriage is for a husband and wife to be faithful to each other and, as we saw in the Old Testament, for them to support each other with food, clothing and conjugal love. If these vows are broken then there are grounds for divorce.

Since there is no question that the abusing husband is "neglecting" to support his wife she should be aware that she *does* have the option to divorce him because Paul recognised the validity of divorces when unbelievers neglected their partners. And this also applies to Christians who break marriage vows – just because Paul did not expect Christians to act in this way does not mean they are not capable of it; Paul simply expected them to know better.

We should not forget, though, that Jesus emphasised forgiveness, as we saw in chapter 5, so we should not advise this woman to divorce her husband the first time he breaks his vows. However, if he continues to sin hard-heartedly (i.e. stubbornly or without repentance) Jesus said she may divorce him. In practice we have to depend on the individual concerned to decide when enough is enough, because we cannot know what goes on inside a marriage. We cannot know how much emotional abuse is happening and even physical abuse is largely unseen or unreported.

## Behind the façade

We will never know how many of our friends return home to desperately sad and perhaps even dangerous situations. The façade of a 'happy' marriage is often perpetuated by the whole family because they are ashamed to admit anything is wrong. A highly respected and successful man may return home to harangue or beat his wife and children, and a modest, quiet woman may meet a lover regularly or attack her husband with hurtful spite at every opportunity. But these are stereotypes and no-one who looks from the outside can guess what is   really happening behind a front door.

One man told me, rather shamefaced, about his former wife who was outwardly a respectable and demure woman but inside the home she always got her way and had a terrible temper. If she felt that her husband wasn't prompt enough to do what she demanded, she would shout and hit out with whatever was at hand. He was brought up not to hit women, so he just tried to defend himself while she continued striking him till her temper subsided or she got tired. On three occasions she broke his arm which he had held up in defence. Once she managed to break his leg – though I'm not sure how – and he never told the hospital staff what had actually happened.

He didn't divorce his wife because he thought a Christian should not divorce on the grounds of abuse. During one hospital admission a friend from a different church pointed out that one day she was likely to kill him and God couldn't possibly mean that to happen. He took this friend's advice and left her and eventually divorced her. When he did this, his church rejected him because they didn't know anything about the violence and they regarded his wife as a victim of a completely groundless divorce. The story has a happy ending – he found a new wife and they enjoy a wonderful life together. The Lord has certainly blessed his new marriage and they are both very active workers in another church.

Another true example of a false façade is of a minister of a large church who frequently abused his wife. She was injured badly enough to need to go to hospital on more than one occasion. His ministry was blessed by many conversions and a thriving congregation, but his happy family life was a sham. Few people know what his wife went through, but God knows.

Only the Lord really knows the heart and, as Jesus said, evil comes from within and loves the dark. We cannot leave it up to a minister or a church leadership to decide when a marriage ends – it is up to the individual victim, in prayer before the Lord. Only they and the Lord know what their life is really like. Only they know if their partner has expressed repentance and only they will have to live with the consequences of the decision.

## To conclude: God knows our secret suffering

Our Lord knows the troubles we face in secret in our own homes, things we never let others see because we are ashamed. People often feel that they have somehow caused their partner to be abusive or to commit adultery, and sometimes this may be partially true, but it does not excuse them. Often we can do things to heal the situation, but sometimes we cannot, and our Lord knows that too.

God has given us a very realistic law in the Old Testament and he did not throw it away when Jesus came to transform us. We are not all transformed yet, and our world is still sinful until the Kingdom fills the earth, and everyone bends the knee to Jesus. Until then, we still need some of the God-given laws of the Old Testament: laws about murder, about injury, about marital neglect and abuse. The details do not always transfer well from one society to another, but Jesus highlighted the principles and generalised them for us (as we saw in detail in chapter 4).

"God is not a ruler who sits on a high throne in isolation, ignorant of the suffering of his people. He aches with us, even in divorce, which he too has suffered. God loves you, and knows your secret sufferings. He wants to help you, and has given us practical laws to help deal with your hurt." *That* is what we say to a person in a neglectful or abusive marriage.

## Further Reading

### *Divorce for neglect allowed by Shammaites and other Jews*

Chapter 5 "Rabbinic teaching" in my *Divorce and Remarriage in the Bible* (Eerdmans, 2002) summarises the evidence from ancient Jewish sources.

### *Four grounds for divorce in Paul*

Chapter 7 "Paul's teaching" in my *Divorce and Remarriage in the Bible* (Eerdmans, 2002) goes through the Biblical text in much more detail.

# 9

# Can I Get Married Again?

## A valid divorce implies the right to remarry

We have seen that Jesus and Paul condemned the easy groundless divorces, but what did they say about remarriage? This is a very difficult issue for Christians mainly because the New Testament says so little. Jesus appears to condemn remarriage – though, as we saw in chapter 5, he was only condemning it after an invalid divorce. Paul is virtually silent on the issue, but there are two good reasons for believing that he allowed remarriage. First, we will see that everyone in the 1st century believed that divorcees could remarry – in fact, most people thought that they *should* remarry – and Paul says nothing to counter this belief. Second, we will see that while Paul does not say 'divorcees can remarry', some of his teaching is based on the assumption that they can.

## Mary's and Joseph's divorce certificate

Did you know that we have found a divorce certificate of Mary and Joseph? It is dated AD 72 so it was not *the* Mary and Joseph, who would have been about 100 years old by that date. 'Mary' was the most popular female name of the time and 'Joseph' was the second most popular male name, so it was likely that there were an awful lot of couples called Mary and Joseph. This particular couple were among a handful of Jews who were living in Masada during the final war against the Romans.

Masada was an impregnable fortress built by Herod the Great on top of a high rocky outcrop which was surrounded by steep sides. The only access was by a single very steep and easily defended path, so Herod made a safe and very comfortable haven for himself and a few privileged individuals. He had huge food stores and underground water cisterns the size of large basements. There were buildings for his servants and a beautifully decorated palace for himself. He even had a luxurious bath-house with an under-floor heating system. When he died, the Romans left a small garrison there but did not develop it in any way.

In AD 66 the Romans invaded Palestine to put down a Jewish revolt. They besieged Jerusalem and eventually destroyed it in AD 70, but some Jews had the foresight to capture Masada and fortify it against the Roman invasion. They managed to defend Masada till AD 73 when the Romans finished the huge task of building an artificial slope against one of the sheer cliff sides of the fortress and then rolled their tall war engines up to the walls.

The Romans found not just soldiers, but whole families in the fortress, who all killed themselves to avoid being captured – men, women and children. The Jews had converted the fortress into a small village and had filled the food stores, adapted one of the buildings into a synagogue with a school, and used a wall tower for a bakery. They settled down and lived there in as normal a way as possible – within the constraints of being under siege by the Romans. People got married there, had children there, and even got divorced there. We know this because some of them hid their most valuable documents and among these was the divorce certificate of Joseph and Mary dated AD 72.

## "You are free to marry any man you wish"

This ancient document followed the traditional wording, including the only words which were compulsory in a Jewish divorce certificate: "You are free to marry any Jewish man you wish." These words are also found in many Greek certificates and convey the legal principle that the reason a divorce certificate was given to a woman was to enable her to remarry.

Everyone in the 1st century, so far as we know, agreed that a divorcee had the right to remarry. The Romans had this right enshrined in their law, and they certainly did not want to introduce any restriction to it and, as far as we know, there were no Jewish parties in the 1st-century who prohibited remarriage after divorce.

## What the Dead Sea Scrolls really say

Some scholars thought at first that the writers of the Dead Sea Scrolls disapproved of remarriage because one of the first of the Scrolls to be discovered, the *Damascus Document*, appeared to say that you should not get married a second time.[23]

The Scrolls of the community at Qumran were discovered in 1947 by an Arab boy looking for treasure. He was deliberately throwing stones into a cave high up in the cliff and the sound of breaking pottery was exactly what he was hoping to hear. He did not climb up to it himself because he was afraid that the treasure might be protected by a *djinn* ("genie") who had been released when he broke the pot, so he enlisted the help of his brother and a friend, by pretending that they were better climbers than him. He said that he would wait at the bottom, "ready to run for help" if there was a *djinn*. The boys were most disappointed when they found nothing more than scrappy documents, but they managed to sell a large scroll to an antique dealer in the market for a few dollars. This dealer recognised that it was a scroll of Isaiah so he showed it to an Orthodox priest who bought it for $70. The priest realised that it was an ancient script and sold it later for a million dollars – which shows the value of learning ancient Hebrew!

The text called the *Damascus Document* describes how a group of Jews deliberately chose to live in the desert to get away from a corrupt priesthood and from other Jews whom they believed did not follow God's law properly. One of the things they criticised was the practice of having more than one wife at a time. Like Jesus, they said that God's plan for marriage was for it to be between one man and one wife, but early scholars misunderstood this passage and thought that they were criticising divorce and remarriage. We now know that this was wrong because other scrolls show that they allowed divorce and it has become clear that the *Damascus Document* was criticising polygamy rather than remarriage – though some older books still repeat the early misunderstanding of this text. The Jews at Qumran, like all other Jews, regarded remarriage as the right of any divorcee.

## Everyone expected divorcees to remarry

Actually both Jews and Romans in the 1st century thought that most divorcees *should* remarry. A Roman citizen who did not get remarried within 18 months of a divorce (or within 2 years if their partner had died) could be prosecuted under a law which was enacted by the Emperor Augustus in 18 BC. Augustus was concerned that many young men were avoiding marriage by divorcing the brides their parents had arranged for them to marry, and then living care-free and licentious lives. He was also concerned that there were not enough children being born to Roman citizens, so he wanted these young men to get remarried and have more children.

Jews also thought that divorcees *should* remarry, especially child-less ones, because they had not yet obeyed the command: "Be fruit-ful and multiply". They believed it was the duty of every Jewish man to have at least two children in order to fulfil this command and, if they had not done so before they were divorced or widowed, they were expected to remarry.

Remarriage for divorcees in the 1st century was therefore the norm – if they did not do so they were contravening the secular or religious law. And they all knew that they had the right to remarry because it was written into their divorce certificates: "You may marry any man you wish. "

## Paul quotes a divorce certificate

These words, which were so well known from Jewish and Graeco-Roman divorce certificates, are found in the New Testament, where Paul quotes a Christian version of them:

> 1 Cor. 7.39: "… she is free to be married to whom she wishes, only in the Lord."

When Jews wrote out their divorce certificates they usually added the word "Jewish" so that the words became "you may marry any *Jewish* man you wish". This reminded their ex-wife that she should only remarry within the faith. Paul makes a similar addition by telling Christian widows that they may only remarry "in the Lord" – i.e. a Christian man. We do not know if Paul converted this Jewish formula into a Christian one or whether he was quoting a traditional Christian version, but either way it would be very odd to quote these words if Christians disapproved altogether of remarriage after divorce.

It seems strange at first that Paul used this phrase in v. 39, where he was speaking to widows and not to divorcees but, as we saw in chapter 7, it was because he wanted to assure Christian widows that they did not need to follow the Jewish law of Levirate marriage which would make them marry their brother-in-law if they were childless. Paul argued that a widow should have the same rights as a divorcee; if a divorcee could marry whoever she wished, then a widow should have this same right.

The interesting thing for us is that Paul's reasoning only works if you believe that divorcees *do* have the right to remarry. It would be no good assuring the widows that they had the same rights as divorcees, to remarry anyone they wished, if divorcees were not in fact allowed to re-marry at all. Paul was therefore assuming in this passage that his readers believed divorcees did have the right to remarry.

## Paul says abandoned believers can remarry

The only place where Paul specifically spoke about remarriage is when he addressed the believer who had been abandoned by their partner.

We saw in chapter 6 that separation was equivalent to divorce in Roman law, so that when someone was abandoned by their partner or was asked to leave their partner's house they were divorced by them. Paul was totally against this Roman groundless divorce-by-separation, just as Jesus was against the Jewish groundless divorce, and he told Christians who had separated from their partners that they should try to undo this divorce by attempting a reconciliation and remaining unmarried while they were doing so (v. 11). But what if a believer was the victim of a Roman divorce-by-separation? We saw that Paul told them they were "not enslaved" (v. 15).

Some people interpret 'not enslaved' as meaning 'no longer tied to your partner' (i.e. you can live apart but you cannot divorce), while others interpret it as 'no longer tied to your marriage' (i.e. you can get divorced but not remarry). Both these interpretations would have sounded like nonsense to a 1st-century reader because Paul was speaking to someone who was *already divorced*, so they have no choice in the matter. It was no good telling them that they could live apart because this was already forced on them, and it was no good telling them that they could get divorced because as far as Roman law was concerned they were already divorced.

A 1st-century reader of Paul's letter would have had no doubt about what 'not enslaved' meant, because it would remind them about the words on their divorce certificate: "you are now free to marry". Even if they did not have a divorce certificate (because many Roman divorces took place without an actual certificate) they would still have this right in Roman law. Paul would have been understood to be saying very clearly, 'You are no longer enslaved – you are free from that marriage and, as any divorce certificate says, free to remarry.'

Paul granted this freedom to a believer who was separated because their unbelieving partner had deserted them, but not to the believer who had separated from their partner. He did not approve of this groundless divorce and if the believer had done the separating, he urged them to attempt reconciliation with their partner (1 Cor. 7.11). However, when someone was the victim of a Roman divorce-by-separation they were powerless to reverse the situation, so Paul allowed them to regard their divorce as valid.

## Abandonment is 'neglect'

What was Paul's justification for regarding this type of div-orce as valid for the victim? On the face of it he was being inconsistent. He was saying on the one hand that divorce-by-separation was an invalid form of divorce but on the other hand he allowed the victim to remarry – which implies that he did think it was valid. There are two possible answers: he is either being legalistic or pragmatic.

Paul could be pointing out that the victims had been des-erted and, as we have seen, under Jewish law they would then have a right to a divorce because they were suffering neglect as defined in Exodus 21.10–11 – i.e. their partner was failing to provide food, clothing and conjugal love. It is likely that this was in Paul's mind because speaking about being "enslaved" is a little strange in the context of marriage but it is natural when speaking about Exodus 21.10 which originally concerned slavery.

Strictly speaking, although it is true that the victim had grounds for a Biblical divorce (neglect), the divorce had not been properly processed according to Jewish custom. However, Paul may have been stating a practical solution which was fair to the victim even if it wasn't legally watertight. We have a very clear indication that Paul was thinking this pragmatic way because he used the phrase "God has called you to peace". This phrase is similar to the Rabbinic legal phrase "for the sake of peace", which is what courts said when they gave a pragmatic solution in a case where a strict application of the law would be unfair. For example, strictly speaking, a child could not be liable for theft, but this would mean that a child could take and keep anything they found. The Rabbinic courts decided that this was stealing, though it would go without punishment. They could not justify this in strictly legal terms, so they made a ruling that was practical and fair. They said: "we do this for the sake of peace," and Paul is saying the same thing, though he says this is God's ruling: "*God* has called you to peace."

Paul probably based his decision on both pragmatism *and* the application of the law of divorce for neglect. Either way, his decision makes good common sense which is fair to the victim, without approving of divorce-by-separation.

## Even the guilty partner can remarry – eventually

Paul allowed the victim of a groundless divorce to get remarried, but what about the person who carries out this divorce? – Can they ever get remarried? On the face of it the answer is 'No', or at least, 'Not for some time'. This is because Paul gives very clear instructions in 1 Corinthians 7.11 that the person who has separated from their partner must remain unmarried and attempt to be reconciled with the person whom they have divorced.

Paul does not say how long someone should continue to remain unmarried and attempt reconciliation, and many interpreters assume that they may never remarry. However, Paul's instruction is not a punishment but an attempt to help the victim of that divorce. He was telling the person who forced their partner into an unwarranted divorce that they should try to put things right by giving their ex-partner the opportunity to continue the marriage – or, strictly speaking, to remarry them. This implies that when it is *no longer possible* to reverse the mistake, the command is no longer in force, because it can no longer be carried out. If the divorced partner marries someone else or rejects all the attempts at reconciliation, then we can assume that the person can stop trying for reconciliation and they can remarry.

It would certainly be strange if the command not to re-marry was a punishment for groundless divorce because this would make it into an unforgivable sin and we know that there is only one of these (Mt. 12.31). One might argue that the inability to remarry was a consequence but not a punishment, because the former marriage is still carrying on in some spiritual way or in God's eyes. This reasoning only works if no-one can remarry after a divorce, because if the innocent victim can remarry (as we have concluded in this book) then the marriage is over. We saw in chapter 7 that the concept that only death can end a marriage is not Scriptural and is based on a misunderstanding of a few texts.

Therefore the command that the 'guilty' partner should avoid remarriage is not a consequence nor a punishment but a practical way in which they can try to reverse their mistake, and the command only lasts as long as this might still be possible. In practice, few people who divorce someone against their will would bother to obey this command unless, like these Corinthians, they were convicted that they had done something wrong soon after the divorce. But what if they were convicted of this long after they had divorced, when one or both of them had already remarried? Should they attempt to divorce their new partner in order to be reconciled and remarry their original partner? We will look at this in the next chapter.

## To conclude: Paul allows remarriage

I am sure that if Paul had told Christians that they should never remarry they would have obeyed, even though it meant breaking the Roman law and putting them in danger of prosecution, and even if they did not yet have any children so that they were breaking the Jewish laws of piety. Just as some of them were willing to face lions and torturers because they refused to say that 'Caesar is Lord', I am sure that they would have been willing to break the laws which commanded remarriage – *if* Paul had told them to.

We have seen in previous chapters that Jesus and Paul only told those who had invalid divorces to avoid remarriage, which implies that those who had valid divorces were allowed to remarry. In this chapter we found that Paul's teaching *assumes* that divorcees can remarry but we are still left with the fact that Jesus and Paul did not *specifically* say that divorcees may remarry. Can we safely assume that they can, simply based on this silence?

Silence on this issue is not strange, and actually it would be more strange if Paul specifically allowed divorcees to remarry, because the question never arose in the 1st century. It would be like Paul saying "married women may have children" or "a married couple may sleep in the same bed" – there was no need to say it because it was the nature and purpose of marriage. There was even less reason to say that "a divorced person may remarry" because not only was the right of remarriage regarded as the very nature of divorce, but they also had a legal certificate which said precisely this. If we said that Paul's silence means that he condemned remarriage, then we would also have to assume that his silence condemned breast-feeding by Christians or celebrating birthdays or adopting children or any number of things which were considered as normal activities by everyone in the ancient world.

We therefore have to conclude that Paul allowed validly divorced believers to remarry. If they *had* used the invalid Roman divorce-by-separation he told them they should not remarry but try to reverse the divorce instead, but if they were a *victim* of this kind of divorce they could not do anything to reverse it so they could regard it as a valid divorce based on neglect. Paul even quoted the words of the divorce certificate with approval and his words 'not enslaved' would be unambiguous to a 1st-century reader.

His teaching on remarriage is admittedly ambiguous to modern readers and we will look in chapter 12 at the reasons why our perception has changed so dramatically. Before that, however, we have to look at the difficult situation of those who *have* divorced but they cannot say that their divorce was based on Biblical grounds.

## Further Reading

### *Early Jewish divorce certificates*

My academic article "1 Corinthians 7 in the light of the Jewish Greek and Aramaic Marriage and Divorce Papyri" (*Tyndale Bulletin*, 52, 2001, 225–43) analyses some typical documents from the first two centuries.

Chapter 5 "Rabbinic Teaching" in my *Divorce and Remarriage in the Bible* (Eerdmans, 2002) examines especially the Masada divorce certificate in the light of Rabbinic teaching.

### *Discoveries at Masada*

*Her Price is beyond Rubies: The Jewish Woman in Greco-Roman Palestine* by Leone J. Archer (Sheffield Academic Press, 1990), who was the first to give English translations of all the important divorce and marriage certificates from Masada and the Judaean desert, as well as discussing the whole subject.

*Masada: Herod's Fortress and the Zealots' Last Stand* (Cardinal, 1973) by Yigael Yadin, who did much of the original excavation, is a colourful and readable account of the history of the site.

### *Paul allowing remarriage*

Chapter 7 "Paul's Teaching" in my *Divorce and Remarriage in the Bible* (Eerdmans, 2002) looks at the Pauline texts in more detail than here.

*...And Marries Another: Divorce and Remarriage in the Teaching of the New Testament* by Craig Keener (Hendrickson, 1991) is very good at presenting Paul's teaching in the light of the Graeco-Roman world.

# Is Remarriage Adultery?

**Don't re-divorce, because 'two wrongs don't make a right'**

We have dealt with Jesus, and Paul's teaching about remarriage after a Biblically valid divorce, but we are now faced with another question. Does a person whose divorce was not Biblically valid have to stay unmarried for the rest of their life? Didn't Jesus say that remarriage after an invalid divorce was committing adultery? And what if you have already got married after an invalid divorce? Are you supposed to get divorced from this new marriage because remarriage is not allowed?

## Joseph's plan to divorce Mary

Nativity plays are invitations to disaster. You will probably be familiar with the story of how the little boy playing the innkeeper got his revenge for not being given the part of Joseph. He opened the door with a triumphant smile: "Of course, there's room – come on in!" Or how about the Joseph who looked disgustedly inside the inn door and replied, "I wouldn't let Mary stay in this dump anyway – we'll be much better off in the stable." Another church in north London decided to add authenticity by using a real oil lamp and real straw. Predictably, a child knocked over the lamp which set fire to the straw, and the authenticity of the scene had to be sacrificed by the use of a modern fire extinguisher. As a local newspaper reported, "No children were hurt but baby Jesus melted."

The real Christmas story had to cope with many more potential disasters. The wise men might have returned to Herod or his soldiers may have arrived before Jesus' family left Bethlehem. God had to employ his angels in a role similar to that of a stage prompter in order to avoid these disasters. The first potential calamity to be averted by an angel was when Joseph nearly divorced his betrothed wife Mary for her seeming infidelity. Joseph considered using an 'Any Cause' divorce and chose this type of divorce for the best of reasons – he wanted to avoid putting Mary to shame in a public court (Mt. 1.19). But as we saw in chapter 5, Jesus taught that the 'Any Cause' divorce was invalid and so the first nativity story almost started and ended with an invalid divorce!

### An invalid divorce for valid reasons

Joseph was planning to use the 'Any Cause' divorce in order to save Mary's shame, but would this have meant that he had an invalid divorce? In our modern day we have many similar situations where a divorce is granted without citing any specific fault because the adulterous partner has agreed not to contest the divorce. Similarly, someone who is suffering abuse may separate from their partner and later get a divorce based on that separation, without actually saying anything about the abuse in the divorce petition. Would we therefore conclude that the innocent partner has a Biblically invalid divorce in these situations because they had not got divorced on valid Biblical grounds?

We saw a similar type of situation in the previous chapter where Paul recognised a divorce as valid even though no Biblical grounds were cited to enact it. This was the case of someone who was the victim of a divorce-by-separation. Paul looked behind the divorce to see what had actually *caused* it, i.e. the Biblical grounds of neglect when they were abandoned, and recognised that even if the divorce procedure did not actually name the Biblical ground, it was, nonetheless, the reason for it. He therefore told the innocent partner that they were "not enslaved" (1 Cor. 7.15) so that they could divorce and remarry.

### Invalid divorce for no good reason

If a divorce *was* invalid and the divorcee has remarried, should they now divorce their second partner and return to their first in order to put things right? Many people think that they should do so, and some have even done it, but since this results in yet another marriage break-up (of the second marriage) it is difficult to justify.

If anyone *did* act on this teaching and divorce their new husband or wife it would be like trying to put right a wrong by committing another wrong. 'Two wrongs don't make a right', as they say, and the injury caused by breaking one set of marriage vows cannot be healed by doing the same wrong to someone else.

It is like a person who hears an ecologist say: "If you have hardwood kitchen fittings you are helping to destroy valuable rain forests," so they tear out their expensive mahogany kitchen cupboards and replace them with pine ones. This drastic action does not help anyone and merely results in utterly wasting the valuable mahogany. The ecologist expressed his message in this dramatic way to get attention and to bring home the importance and relevance of the subject, but he did not expect anyone to tear out their kitchen fittings because this would not help the situation and simply compounds the mistake.

Jesus made a similarly dramatic statement when he said, "If you have remarried after an invalid divorce, you are committing adultery". He was pointing out the serious implications of an invalid divorce in the most forceful way possible. He said, in effect, "No one can ignore the invalidity of 'Any Cause' divorces because, technically, anyone who remarries after one is committing adultery." The Gospel writers do not record the word "technically", however, and I do not think that Jesus would have used a word like this because it dilutes the shock of the message. It makes far more impact to say, 'if you re-marry you *are* an adulterer'.

## Preacher's rhetoric

Preachers often make similar statements. They say things like: "If you do not share the Gospel with your neighbour, you are opening the door to hell for them," or "Looking at pornog-raphy is committing adultery against your wife." (This second example is based on what Jesus said in Matthew 5.28: "everyone who looks at a woman with lustful intent has already committed adultery with her in his heart".) Another such bold declaration made by Jesus is: "everyone who is angry with his brother will be liable to judgment" for murder (Mt. 5.22). He did not mean, however, that this person should be punished as if they had committed murder and neither did he mean that a person should be punished for adultery if they had looked at someone lustfully or if they had remarried after a technically invalid divorce.

Some people in the early church did take this kind of preaching by Jesus literally, including the teaching "If your right eye causes you to sin, tear it out" (Mt. 5.29). In the early 2nd century a man called Democritus did this and Tertullian had to warn other Christians not to copy his example (*Apology* 46.11–12). Another 2nd-century Church Father, Origen, actually castrated himself in order to fulfil the command, "If your right hand causes you to sin, cut it off and throw it away. For it is better that you lose one of your members than that your whole body go into hell." Paradoxically, later in life he interpreted this same text with a non-literal rhetorical meaning.

It seems self-evident that Jesus is using preacher's rhetoric here and does not expect us to act on it literally. If we did literally follow all of Jesus' rhetorical teachings we would have to put the man who loses his temper in prison and tell the wife of someone who looks lustfully at another woman that she has grounds for divorce, as well as maiming a large proportion of Christians.

These examples of preaching rhetoric were gathered by Matthew into a single passage in Matthew 5.21–32 ending with the teaching that remarriage after invalid divorce is adultery. It follows immediately after Jesus said that lust is adultery and that we should 'cut off' the member which leads to lust. By putting Jesus' saying about remarriage in this context, Matthew was clearly implying that Jesus was not speaking in a literal way. He did not expect anyone to act as though remarriage was literally adultery any more than he expected them to act as though *lust* was literally adultery.

## No-one said: Get divorced again

The specific words which Jesus used make it clearer still that he did not expect us to carry out a divorce because although he said about the roving eye "...tear it out" and about the erring hand "...cut it off", he did *not* say to the remarried, "...get divorced". If we do not literally act on the commands which Jesus *did* say ("tear it out" and "cut it off"), it is cert-ainly wrong that we should presume to act on the command which Jesus did *not* say ("get divorced").

Paul must also have come across this problem on many occasions because a large number of converts would have been remarried divorcees. Roman citizens walked in and out of marriages frequently, and virtually all of their divorces would have been without valid grounds. Paul did not say anything in any of his letters to people in this situation, which presumably means that he did not think they needed to do anything. As we saw in chapter 9, he took a very practical approach to the situation of believers who had been abandoned by their partners, telling them that they were "not enslaved" because "God has called you to peace", and he probably applied the same pragmatism to this situation. In other words he treated their invalid divorce as if it was actually valid on the pragmatic grounds that the remarried divorcee could not now put things right.

Therefore, although Jesus pointed out that virtually all Jewish remarriages were technically adulterous, neither he nor Paul told these remarried couples to get divorced or to try to rectify the situation any other way.

## Invalid divorces before conversion

Some churches say that a new Christian starts their life from scratch, so that an invalid divorce which they had before they became a Christian does not count. This is based on the assumption that any vows which they made before they became Christians were not taken before God so they do not carry the same force.

This view implies that God disregards the vows of non-Christians and that marriages by non-Christians are somehow less valid. It also implies that their present marriage may be substandard in some way because they made their vows while they were still non-Christians. Although most churches which have this type of policy would, nonetheless, affirm the validity of marriage vows by non-Christians, it is still true that their standpoint assumes that vows made before a person became a Christian are allowed to be broken whereas vows by Christians cannot.

This is similar to the way in which some of the people in Corinth were thinking, and Paul was keen to correct them. When they became Christians they started to regard their former life with contempt and, for some of them, this included their marriage partner. They consequently thought that they should divorce their non-believing partner in order to be better Christians but Paul told them they were not allowed to do this (1 Cor. 7.12–14). He said that if their unbelieving partner was willing to stay married, the Christian partner should certainly not be the one who breaks up the marriage because God recognised a marriage to non-believers just as much as a marriage between two believers.

Paul told Christians to remain with their non-Christian partners if it was at all possible and he did not regard a marriage which was

contracted before they became Christians as any less permanent than
one which was contracted after. He did say that if the unbelieving
partner wanted to leave then the believer should let them do so. This
did not imply that breaking up a marriage to a non-believer was less
terrible than breaking up a marriage between two believers but
simply that they had to let an unbeliever leave because there wasn't
anything which they could do to stop them.

When we become a Christian we are a new creation and we start
from scratch without any sin, but we do not start from scratch with
regard to our marriages and other commitments such as loans or
business contracts. We should be even *more* committed to keeping
promises and vows which we made when we were not Christians.

## Deciding innocence or guilt

Although we have found that remarriage is possible even after an
invalid divorce, this does not minimise the sin of breaking up the
previous marriage. Like any sin, it can be repented of and forgiven,
but some churches will consider that this sin is so serious that they
will refuse to remarry the guilty partner after a divorce, or either
partner after a groundless divorce.

I do not agree with this position because, as I said at the end of the
previous chapter, I think that a church should remarry someone even
if they had forced an innocent partner into a divorce – though only
after they have gone back to their former partner with a genuine
offer of reconciliation and have truly repented of this sin. But I can
appreciate that some churches will not want to remarry such people
on their premises and this is, of course, a perfectly valid decision for
them to make. However, churches which do have policies which are
based on innocence or guilt in a divorce need some kind of procedure for deciding what actually caused the break-up of the marriage.

It is very difficult to decide guilt and innocence without a court
trial because without the formalities of evidence and cross-examina-
tion it is usually the loudest person who gets their viewpoint heard
and the other partner is often unable to present their side of the story.
But even if the divorce goes to trial, a secular court does not decide
guilt on the Biblical basis of breaking marriage vows and so the
church is still left without any authoritative decision.

In some churches the elders or bishop may wish to inves-tigate the
divorce, though as I suggested at the end of chapter 8, it is very difficult for others to really know what takes place in private behind the

façade of a normal marriage. I have come across too many instances where the innocent partner is ostracised by a church – wives of highly respected ministers who, in private, are abusive or unfaithful, or husbands who are assumed to be guilty of some unknown sin because their wives have walked out on them. Only God can reliably judge who is the guilty and who is the innocent partner. In any case, by the time most marriages break up, both partners have broken their vows to support each other.

My own practice therefore is not to attempt to judge who is innocent and who is guilty. I feel that it is better to leave justice and forgiveness to God. This does not mean that we should ignore the sin of breaking up the marriage, but we should remember that we are not the ones against whom the sin has been committed. The person who breaks their marriage vows has sinned against their partner and against God before whom those vows were made, and they should ask forgiveness from both of them. I therefore always have a Service of Repentance for broken promises before any marriage involving a divorcee – as explained in the next chapter.

## To conclude: Divorce is forgivable

We have seen that the sin of marriage break-up is very serious but God forgives a repentant divorcee just as he forgives all other sinners. That does not mean that there will not be consequences to suffer as a result of this sin – because all divorces cause suffering and the suffering from a marriage break-up can last a lifetime – but it does mean that the consequences of the sin can stop getting worse. Therefore a remarried divorcee should not divorce his or her new partner, because this would be the cause of even more suffering. Interpreting Jesus' words in this way is as erroneous as concluding that we should cut off parts of our body that cause us to sin.

Our God is a loving Father who knows the failings of his children. He knows the foolish and self-destructive things we do and he helps us to prevent them and brings healing afterwards. He offers us wisdom in his Word, warning us not to break marriage vows, then he tells us to reverse our foolishness if it is still possible. And even when it is no longer possible to put right the wrong which we have done, he still offers us forgiveness and leads us forward.

# 11

# Promises, Promises

### Marriage vows and remarriage in church

When you sign a contract, do you read the small print? We know we should, but it's such a chore that we usually don't bother. What about when you got married? Did you read the small print then? Perhaps you did not realise there was any, because the small print in a marriage service consists of the marriage vows. You promise to love, honour and keep, and perhaps to obey. The wording varies, but it has remained remarkably similar for centuries and we can trace the vows right back to the Old Testament.

## The earliest English marriage service

One vow *has* changed, because in the earliest English marriage services the bride's vows included a promise to be:

> "bonny and buxom in bed and at board."

This wonderfully alliterative phrase comes from the *Use of Sarum*, the earliest English marriage service I have found, which was authorised by the Bishop of Salisbury in 1085. In this very early version some of the vows were still in Latin while others were in old English. The whole service is almost identical with our modern version except that the Latin has been translated and the line about bonny and buxom brides has been omitted.

Originally these words meant something rather different from now. "Bonny" is from the French '*bon*', or 'good'; "buxom" is from an old German word meaning 'pliant' or 'obedient'; "board" is where you put food (on the 'sideboard') so this means mealtimes; and "bed" simply meant 'night-time'. So "Be bonny and buxom in bed and at board" meant: "Behave properly and obediently through night and day." The meanings of these words changed over the years and the church objected to talking about bonny and buxom brides in bed, so we have now lost this vow.

The other marriage vows have survived intact and this is very fortunate because they come from the New Testament. Both bride and groom make promises to each other that they will "love, honour, and keep" or "love, nourish and cherish" or something equivalent. The exact words vary, but these basic ideas are always present because they come from Ephesians:

> Eph. 5.28–29: Husbands should love their wives as their own bodies. He who loves his wife loves himself. [29] For no-one ever hated his own flesh, but **nourishes** and **cherishes** it, just as Christ does the church.

## Our marriage vows come from Exodus 21

Paul said that husbands should love, nourish and cherish their brides like Christ loves, nourishes and cherishes the church. He was saying that Christ keeps the same marriage vows with regard to the church which a groom makes to his bride. The words translated "nourishes and cherishes" mean "to feed" and "to keep warm". They are intimate words which usually describe feeding and caring for children or other loved ones and Paul was therefore saying that every groom should love, feed and clothe his wife – which are exactly the same three obligations which we found in Exodus 21.10.

These same vows were expressed in a wider variety of language in Jewish marriage contracts. As well as intimate terms like "nourish" and "cherish" they also used more general terms like "care for" and "honour" instead of "feed and clothe". Christian marriages also employ a wide variety of language, perhaps partly through the influence of the synagogue which also influenced the language of Ephesians. All these variations in both Christian and Jewish marriages can be traced back to the wording of Exodus 21.10.

Christian wedding services preserved these vows more accurately than Jewish marriage contracts, especially concerning the vow of 'conjugal love' – for example, when it included the beautiful phrase "with my body I worship you".

All three vows were expressed in 1st and 2nd-century Jewish marriage certificates, where bride and groom promised each other "food, clothing and bed", but later Jewish marriage certificates omit even this coy reference to conjugal activity. However, Jewish marriage contracts are very useful for tracing the gradual change from a straightforward quotation of Exodus 21.10 "food and clothing and conjugal love" to more general terminology like "care for" and "honour".

## Valuable contracts in the rubbish room

The best collection of early Jewish marriage contracts comes from a huge collection of documents which were rescued from a rubbish room in the Cairo synagogue by two women in the 1890s. Dr Agnes Smith Lewis and Dr Margaret Dunlop Gibson were twin sisters who became two of the most remarkable female scholars in Biblical studies. When they had both been widowed they set off on a tour of the Middle East where their ability to read ancient texts in Hebrew, Greek, Syriac and Arabic made them welcome even in male-only establishments like the library of the Sinai Monastery. It was here that they recognised and rescued a vellum page from a valuable 5th-century Gospel in Old Syriac which was being used as a butter dish. Another great discovery were original Hebrew manuscripts of Ecclesiasticus which till then was only known in its Greek translation. It was this discovery which led them to the Cairo Synagogue and its sacred rubbish room or 'Geniza'.

A Geniza was where Jews deposited all the documents and books which were no longer wanted but which could not be thrown away because they contained the written name of God. These included any Scripture text which had become worn or damaged, which had to be thrown away to prevent any mistakes being made while reading it. They also threw private contracts, such as wills or documents of marriage or divorce, into a Geniza because these, too, contained the name of God. Every few years they emptied a Geniza by putting all the documents and books in a coffin and burying them with a full Jewish funeral service.

The Geniza at Cairo was special because it had been ne-glected and had not been emptied for about a thousand years! With the help of Dr Solomon Schechter the women got the permission of the synagogue authorities to take the most valuable of these documents for scholars to study in Cambridge. They filled several tea-chests with so many documents that Cambridge University Library has only recently finished the huge job of cataloguing and preserving them all, and many are still awaiting detailed study.

Recent studies of the marriage contracts in this Geniza collection have clearly shown that the origin of the words "honour" and "care for" or "keep" or "cherish" can be traced back to the vows to feed and clothe in Exodus 21.

## The vow "to obey"

The vow to obey, which is found in most Jewish and Christian marriages, is very different from the other marriage vows: it is not found in Exodus 21; it is not referred to anywhere else in the Old Testament as a marriage vow; and it is one-sided, because usually only the woman promises it.

Did you or your partner promise to obey when you got married? Perhaps you were not listening to that part of the marriage service and you can't remember what promises you made to each other! Some services include 'obey' and others omit it. When I conduct a marriage service I always give couples the choice to include it or not and ask them to decide together long before the wedding which vows each of them will make. Their consideration of this issue sometimes produces heated debates and even arguments! But it is better to argue about this and other presuppositions *before* you get married than wake up on your first morning at home and argue about who is making the breakfast!

If you do not have any problems with the vow to obey you can skip the next couple of sections. Some people insist on this vow while others regard it as un-Christian. If you have already made up your mind, I cannot go into enough detail here to change your viewpoint, though you might be interested to know the historic *reasons* for the New Testament teaching.

## Roman women rebelled against submission

The vow of obedience originates in Greek moral regulations and not in the Old Testament law because although women submitted in practice to their husbands in most Old Testament cultures, it only became a *moral rule* in Greek culture. This rule was also important in Roman times and it gained huge importance during the 1st century AD (during the time of the New Testament), because issues of women's rights were starting to get out of hand.

Roman women began to seek more and more rights and to demand that they should have all the same freedoms which the men had, including the freedom to be sexually immoral. They took lovers like their husbands, got drunk like their husbands, and squandered money like their husbands. While their husbands wasted money on chariot racing and on buildings which aggrandised their reputations, their wives spent huge sums on jewellery and hairstyling. This longing for freedom also started to spread to children and slaves, so that children demanded to have whatever they wanted and slaves went on strike. Soon the whole of 'decent' society felt threatened by this drive for freedom.

Moral philosophers tried to stop the rot by harking back to the good old days as epitomised in the writings of Aristotle. He was the great philosopher who taught that society is built on the foundation of the family, with the man as the head of the household. The wife should submit to him as her husband; the children should submit to him as their father; and the household slaves should submit to him as their master. When everyone submitted to the head of the house, conflict would disappear and the whole of society would be harmonious. The Romans regarded this philosophy as a way of coping with the moral breakdown of their society. Women who obeyed did not get drunk or take lovers; children who obeyed were diligent to listen to the slaves who tutored them; and slaves who obeyed did not steal or go on strike.

Most respectable women were appalled by the excesses of the 'freedom' movement so they were careful to show their submissiveness to their husband, in public at least. A woman who exercised her freedom by not being submissive was assumed to be free in her morality too. This was a prejudice, of course, but it is like many people nowadays who assume that a woman who goes into a bar by herself has an immoral lifestyle so, to avoid this type of assumption, many women avoid bars. The only way for a woman to evade similar suspicions of immorality in the 1st century was to be submissive to her husband or father, and the only generally accepted concept of a moral household was a submissive one.

Moral tracts from all branches of society, including Judaism and the Isis religion, urged their adherents to follow this three-fold code of submission by wives, children and slaves in order to demonstrate that they were living moral lifestyles. The New Testament also teaches this three-fold submission, though its authors betray some discomfort with this moral code by adding caveats to it. In Ephesians, for example, we have the familiar Aristotelian list of submission: wives to husbands, children to fathers, and slaves to masters, but each of these has a Christian comment added to it:

Wives should submit *but* husbands should love their wives sacrificially (5.22–33).

Children should submit *but* fathers should not provoke them (6.1–4).

Slaves should submit *but* masters should not threaten them (6.5–9).

This moral code of submission appears in several places in the New Testament, but, again, always with Christian comments added – see 1 Peter 2.18–3.7; 1 Timothy 2.9–15; 6.1–2 and   Colossians 3.18–4.1.

## Why early Christians decided to submit

The New Testament clearly has severe misgivings about this Aristotelean moral code but Christians were, nevertheless, taught to keep it. This was simply because the code defined morality in general society and if Christians ignored it they would give the impression that they were immoral. They therefore decided to follow the code but with some Christian limitations.

Paul explained his motives for teaching Greek morality to Titus and Timothy, who he was training as church leaders. He told Titus that he had to teach women to be "submissive to their own husbands, that the word of God may not be reviled" (Tit. 2.5) – i.e. so that outsiders would not think that Christians were immoral. He said that slaves had to submit to their masters for a similar reason: "Teach slaves to be subject to their masters in everything… so that in every way they will make the teaching about God our Saviour attractive." (Tit. 2.9–10).[24] And he said the same thing to Timothy: "Let all who are under a yoke as slaves regard their own masters as worthy of all honour, so that the name of God and the teaching may not be reviled" (1 Tim. 6.1).

Peter had similar motives, as he explained when he said that wives should submit to their husbands especially if their   husbands were not Christians, because they would be won over by their wives' moral behaviour (1 Pet. 3.1–2). Peter also added that they should avoid other appearances of freedom which 1st-century women were exploiting, such as squandering money on "braiding of hair, the wearing of gold, or the putting on of fine clothing" (v. 3).

Christian women, children and slaves in the 1st century were willing to follow the Aristotelian model of morality in order to avoid slandering the Gospel. Many Christians today continue to follow this moral code, though usually for different reasons. Some today, like the Amish, still avoid jewellery and fine clothes and others still teach submission to husbands and fathers, though of course no-one still teaches submission of slaves. Most modern Christians who follow this lifestyle do so because they regard it is a God-given guide for a harmonious family life. Very few people do it for the same reason as early Christians – that is, in order to aid evangelism.

### Should both brides and grooms promise to "obey"?

We cannot come to a definite conclusion here but it is an important subject for couples to think about together, especially if you have made this vow or are thinking of making it.

If you feel that a vow of obedience should be made I would suggest that the groom as well as the bride should make it. Paul probably had this in mind when he prefaced his words to husbands, wives, children and slaves with the injunction that they should be "submitting to one another" (Eph. 5.21). This was completely opposite to the Aristotelian model where everyone submitted to the father of the house in order to give a clear line of command. Paul said that submission could be a two-way relationship. He emphasised this when he said that   a husband should love his wife sacrificially (Eph. 5:25), that a father should teach his children (a job normally left to slaves) (Eph. 6:4), and that a master should remember that he and his slaves both share the same master in heaven (Eph. 6:9).

In most of the Jewish marriage contracts found in the Cairo Geniza the bride or groom either do not make a vow of obedience at all or it is just made by the bride, but in a few contracts both the bride and groom promise to submit to each other, like Paul suggested. We do not know whether Paul was the first to suggest this, but it is unlikely that Jews would have followed his teaching so perhaps some Jews already practised this mutual submission in the 1st century. Whatever the origin, it is a good model to follow because it has a solid basis in the New Testament while including both concepts of submission and equality. Whatever you decide to include in marriage vows, it should be a joint decision between bride and groom because if they disagree on this, the marriage will not last long.

These vows are among the most serious promises we ever make. They are made before God and in the hearing of the most important people in our lives. Our relatives and friends are not there just as witnesses, but as potential supporters who may help us if our marriage ever starts to go wrong, or if we fall into situations where we are tempted to break our vows. A life-long commitment to another person is difficult and daunting, and we need all the help which others can give us.

Tragically these vows are sometimes broken, and the damage is sometimes so severe that the innocent partner reluctantly decides that the marriage is over. Even more tragically, some marriages are legally dissolved even without broken vows, or the decision to divorce is taken by the guilty partner against the wishes of the innocent one. Should we allow divorcees to repeat the same vows in church to another person?

## When should we refuse remarriage in church?

The traditional reason for forbidding remarriage in church is the belief that a marriage continues, in some mystical way, until a former partner dies. In chapter 7 we found that this traditional church teaching is based on a misunderstanding of a few texts which 1st-century believers would have understood very differently. However, it is understandable that for some churches the history of almost unanimous traditional interpretations may outweigh this insight into how 1st-century believers understood these same texts.

A church could decide to refuse remarriage to anyone who was the guilty partner in a divorce but I don't think this is a practical option because it is often impossible to decide who was guilty and who was innocent. In most cases it is like trying to work out which of two children started a fight. I argued in chapter 10 that Paul probably allowed the guilty partner to remarry if an attempt at reconciliation failed – though this is very uncertain.

There is one situation where a church perhaps *should* refuse conduct a wedding and that is when a divorcee wants to marry the lover with whom they committed adultery. Conducting a wedding in this situation would be like condoning the sin which broke up the former marriage. The early Rabbis actually made an absolute rule to prohibit this, which was very wise and practical because it helped to discourage adultery. It ensured that if your marriage was falling apart and you fell in love with someone else, the *last* thing you would do was commit adultery because it would mean that you could never get married to your lover even if your marriage did end in divorce. Although I cannot find Biblical support for this rule I believe it is certainly worth considering, though unfortunately it won't really be effective unless it becomes generally accepted in all Christian churches.

## Helping divorcees know God's forgiveness

The strongest reason for allowing remarriage in church is that if we refuse it we are saying, on God's behalf, that he does not want that couple to remarry. God forgives sin, and if we really believe this we must also believe that sinners are allowed to move on after repentance. We need to demonstrate that breaking marriage vows is a terrible sin, while at the same time teaching that God is able and willing to forgive this sin.

There is rarely any need to emphasise the sinfulness of marriage break-up to someone remarrying in church, because if you ever find yourself as a bride or groom at the front of a church for the second time, I can guarantee that you will feel guilty. When you have already previously promised to keep your vows "till death us do part" it seems hypocritical to promise the same thing to another person. Even if it was not your fault that the marriage broke down, you may still feel the congregation and even God himself judging you. You know that God understands and that he forgives the repentant sinner, but knowing this still doesn't stop you feeling hypocritical.

I have lived through these feelings with many couples and often someone who was clearly an innocent victim of a divorce feels just as much guilt as a person who caused a break-up. They took their vows seriously the first time and are just as serious this time. They want reassurance that their sins are forgiven and they want God to help them do better this time.

## Service of repentance for broken vows

I have found it very useful to have an informal service of repentance for broken promises shortly before the wedding. In fact I insist on this for all weddings which involve a partner who has been divorced because I have found that those who are most aware of their previous broken vows *want* this service and those who are not sufficiently aware of their guilt *need* it.

I invite both partners to take part in the service of repentance, whether or not they are both divorced, and all three of us ask for God's forgiveness for broken promises because we are all guilty of this at some time. This does not diminish the uniqueness of marriage vows or the seriousness of breaking them, but it does emphasise that *all* sins are serious and all sins are forgivable. This service consists of a short prayer time, perhaps with a   reading. You may find the following prayer useful or you may prepare something similar. It is useful to have the prayer written down so that all three can pray it aloud, together.

> Heavenly Father, who has cared for me from my birth and who has promised to love me unconditionally, I come to you in repentance. I confess that I have made promises to you and to others which I have not kept. I have promised to pray for people or promised to love and care for them and I have not kept these promises as I should. Please forgive me for my sin and give comfort to those whom I have let down and hurt. Give me strength for the future to be able to keep the promises which I will make. I ask you these things in the name of our Lord Jesus, Amen.

This can be followed by the minister praying for the couple's future life together.

The best time and place for this is just after the wedding rehearsal which is usually the day before the wedding in the place where the couple will marry. The rehearsal will probably have made them think about their vows already, so it is an ideal time to ask God to forgive their past and help them with the future. Most Christian divorcees will already have asked God's forgiveness for any part they played in their marriage break-up, so an important aspect of this service is an affir-mation of forgiveness.

Couples have told me that this simple service gave them a real sense of God's forgiveness and that they were able to face their wedding with a clear conscience and with a sense of God's strength to make a success of their new marriage. Although I insist on this service for any marriage involving a divorcee, I have never had to force the issue – everyone has been willing to take part. In fact most of them are very happy to do so and some said that they were relieved that someone had finally taken their former promises seriously.

## To conclude: Marriage vows are the key

Marriage vows are central to the wedding service and the foundation of a life together. Allowing remarriage in church does not diminish their importance, so long as we make sure that there is sufficient recognition that breaking marriage vows is sinful and requires repentance and forgiveness.

The Biblical vows have survived intact from their origins in the book of Exodus, via the Jewish marriage contracts and the letter to the Ephesians and through to the early English marriage services where they have remained almost unchanged for the last thousand years. The language has evolved from "love, clothe and feed" to more general terms like "love, honour and cherish" but the underlying principles have remained the same – material support and physical affection. When we marry, we make these promises to each other, and when we break them, the marriage starts to break down, because when you fail to love or honour or cherish each other, what is left?

The Holy Spirit has ensured that we still make the same marriage vows which God recommended through Moses even though the church has forgotten their origin. It is remarkable that these vows have been preserved when we consider that the church has almost completely forgotten the Biblical principles of marriage and divorce. How did the church forget these vital principles? We will look at this question in the next   chapter.

## Further Reading

### *Geniza documents*

*A Jewish Marriage in Palestine: A Cairo Geniza Study* by Mordechai Friedman (Daf-Chen Press, 1980) collects and analyses most of the mainstream Rabbinic marriage contracts.

*Karaite marriage contracts from the Cairo Geniza: legal training and community life in mediaeval Egypt and Palestine* by Judith Olszowy-Schlanger (Brill, 1998) does the same thing for   marriage contracts of Karaite Jews. These are important because the Karaites were a back-to-the-Bible movement so their contracts often reveal the Biblical basis for older traditions.

### *Early English marriage services*

*A history of the Book of Common Prayer: with a rationale of its offices* by Francis Procter (Macmillan, 1860) is a very old book, but is still a standard work on which others are based.

### Roman women and submission in the 1st century

*Women and Religion in the First Christian Centuries* by Deborah F. Sawyer (Routledge, 1996) and *Women in the Classical World: image and text* edited by Elaine Fantham (Oxford University Press, 1995) are good examples of many books written on this subject by scholars of the classical world.

*Paul, women & wives: marriage and women's ministry in the letters of Paul* by Craig Keener (Hendrickson, 1992) is by a New Testament scholar who is an expert on the Graeco-Roman world.

# 12

# The Teaching which Time Forgot

**Why did the church misunderstand Jesus so soon?**

Almost all of the earliest church leaders, from the 2nd century onwards, believed that Jesus did not allow divorce and only allowed separation in the case of adultery. But as we have seen, anyone in the 1st century would have pointed out that this was a severe misunderstanding of what Jesus and Paul taught, so how could such a huge and drastic mistake have happened after such a short period of time?

## Survival of Judaism after AD 70

The first reason is the cataclysmic destruction of Jerusalem which changed the whole world of Judaism and cut off Christianity from its Jewish roots. When the Romans defeated Jerusalem and destroyed the Temple in AD 70, much of the Jewish world of the New Testament was lost. Most of the Jewish leaders died during the siege and Judaism was never the same again. The fact that Rabbinic Judaism survived at all was remarkable and, according to a traditional story, it was largely due to one man.

Johanan ben Zakkai was a Hillelite Pharisee who was an expert in both Biblical interpretation and Rabbinic law. He escaped from Jerusalem while it was besieged by pretending to be dead so that his disciples could carry him out in a coffin. The Roman guards were stopping everyone who tried to leave the city but they let this small funeral party through, probably helped by a bribe. When they were safely out of sight, Johanan climbed out of the coffin and, instead of escaping, he went to the tent of the Roman commander, Vespasian. He told the commander that Scripture said that the one who conquers Jerusalem will be king, and therefore he prophesied that Vespasian would one day be Emperor. Vespasian was very pleased with this and asked Johanan if he wanted anything. Johanan took his chance and requested the city of Jamnia to be given as a safe place for Jewish scholars, and Vespasian granted the request.

After the war, the surviving Jewish scholars gathered at Jamnia to establish a new centre for Rabbinic law. They called it a 'Sanhedrin' after the religious parliament which had ruled in Jerusalem, though the Judaism which they presided over was very different from the Judaism of the New Testament era. A large number of Jewish groups virtually disappeared after AD 70, including Sadducees, Herodians, Qumran Jews and Shammaite Pharisees. The only type of Jews who had any significant authority in this new age were Hillelite Pharisees, like Johanan. Consequently the Jewish law from then on was interpreted in virtually every respect according to the traditions of the Hillelite school.

It is not surprising therefore that all divorces after this time were based on the Hillelite ground of 'Any Cause' because even though its validity was disputed by Jesus and the Shammaites, as we saw in chapter 5, the Hillelites were the only significant Jewish group to survive after AD 70. It very quickly became the only type of divorce to exist and from then on it was not called an 'Any Cause' divorce but simply a 'divorce'. The whole debate surrounding the legal phrase 'Any Cause' and the Shammaite slogan "nothing except 'Sexual Immorality'" – which was as well-known in early 1st-century Judaism as the term 'maintenance payment' is today – quickly disappeared from public consciousness. Within another couple of centuries these details had become obscure even to scholars.[25]

## Generations divided by language

Not only did the events of AD 70 lead to this misunderstanding of the original legal debate but the evolution of language played its part. Nothing divides generations like language. One generation talks about things being 'spiffing' or 'topping' while another says 'fab' or 'hip', then the next says they are 'fantastic' or 'excellent' and the next says they are 'wicked' or 'cool' One generation says 'we had a gay weekend', and the next says 'don't tell anyone he's gay'. A person with 'learning difficulties' used to be called 'educationally sub-normal' and before that 'mentally handicapped' but earlier still they were referred to by the technical medical term 'imbecile'. Someone from a previous generation could cause serious misunderstanding today by saying, "Isn't it wonderful that so many imbeciles are naturally gay," when what they meant was that those with learning difficulties often have a very cheerful disposition.

Legal jargon changes too, though usually less quickly. For example, if you ask a group of people what a "co-respondent" is, only the older ones among them will remember that it is a legal term for the lover of someone being divorced for adultery. A few decades ago the newspapers regularly had stories about co-respondents and, thanks to human curiosity, these stories were popular reading. When the divorce laws changed in 1967 the term all but disappeared from public consciousness and in another few decades only social historians and readers of historical fiction will know the term. It will be as unknown as the term 'Any Cause' was in the 2nd-century.

Another term which has changed its meaning completely is "intercourse". What would you think of parents who told their daughter, "A young woman should avoid intercourse with men outside her social status"? Nowadays you might say they were libertine snobs, but in the 1800s they would be warning against *speaking* with unsuitable suitors.

The problem with shorthand phrases and assumed knowledge is that different readers have different assumptions. Imagine that you saw some demonstrators with placards reading:

"Equality for women!"

No-one would expect the placard to read:

"We demand equality for women in pay and legal rights!"

Everyone knows that this is what the demonstrator actually means, and if the demonstration was reported in the news-papers the journalist would not bother to spell it out either. However, if this demonstration occurred during the beginning of the 20th century the same slogan would mean something entirely different:

"We demand equality for women in education and voting rights!"

There would be no need, on either occasion, to spell out the whole slogan in a longer version and it would be regarded as rather pedantic to do so. In both contexts it would be obvious what the short slogan meant and the short version would be preferred over the longer one.

In the same way, when Matthew wrote his Gospel there was no need to spell out what 'Any Cause' or "nothing except 'Sexual Immorality'" meant, and a few years earlier, when Mark wrote his Gospel, he did not even feel the need to include these phrases because they would have been too obvious to his readers. As I said in chapter 5, the insertion of these phrases in Mark would seem as pedantic as adding the words 'alcoholic beverages' to the question, "Is it lawful for a 16-year-old to drink?"

However, by the 2nd century, when the legal phrases had been forgotten, the Pharisees' question was understood as "Is it lawful to divorce one's wife for any cause?" – i.e. "is divorce *ever* lawful?" – this was the 'obvious' meaning at that time. No-one spoke about 'Any Cause' divorces any more, not because they didn't exist, but because they were the *only* type of divorce. Similarly today no-one speaks about "co-respondents", not because they do not exist but because they are no longer *mentioned* in divorce cases. 'Intercourse' now always means 'sexual intercourse' and never means 'speaking with'. These examples show that changes in language are still happening and can cause misunderstandings over a couple of generations, even without the complete social upheaval which occurred when the Romans defeated Jerusalem in AD 70.

## Missing punctuation

The church's misinterpretation of Jesus' teaching is further understandable because of the problem caused by translating the original Greek. Try to work out what the following words say:

PHARISEESCAMEUPTOHIMANDTESTEDHIMBYASK
INGISITLAWFULTODIVORCEONESWIFEFORANYCAUSE

Like all New Testament manuscripts up to the 3rd-century this lacks punctuation and is written completely in upper-case letters, without any spaces between the words. You can soon make out the words in the puzzle but to illustrate how the translators could misunderstand it you have to write it down on a piece of paper, making sure that you include the punctuation (go on – have a go).

Probably you have written this sentence in the same way that the vast majority of Bible translations render the Greek:

Pharisees came up to him and tested him by asking, "Is it lawful to divorce one's wife for any cause?"

This is a perfectly good translation of the Greek words, but it does not convey the correct meaning because some essential punctuation is missing. It is better to write it something like:

> Pharisees came up to him and tested him by asking, "Is it lawful to divorce one's wife for 'Any Cause'?"

The addition of quotation marks and upper-case letters to 'Any Cause' is not strictly necessary but it reminds the reader that it is a technical legal phrase. Without this reminder it is very easy to read the question as though the Pharisees were asking Jesus whether divorce is *ever* lawful. This mistake was already being made by the 2nd century, because everyone except Jewish Rabbis had already forgotten that the phrase "'Any Cause' divorce" ever existed.

## God's word can cross the generations

The words of Jesus had to cross many barriers between   the 1st and 2nd-centuries. He spoke to 1st-century Jews in Aramaic, these words were then written down and abbreviated by the Gospel writers, and finally they were translated into Greek for a wider readership. The Christians of the 2nd-century were mainly Gentiles who were living under Roman law, so they had little knowledge of the synagogue or the Hebrew Old Testament. Therefore Jesus' words had to cross the barriers of two or more generations, two completely dissimilar languages and radically different social and legal cultures, so it is not surprising that 2nd-century Christians occasionally misunderstood what he said.

When *we* read the Bible we face similar problems, though by now they have been multiplied many times. We are so far away from the time and culture of the original recipients of these words that sometimes it seems impossible that we will be able to work out what the Holy Spirit was saying to them. Because of this, we often take short cuts to understanding the text, so that when we read a passage of the Bible we tend to ask questions like:

- What is the traditional interpretation of the church?
  *or*
- What is the interpretation of my favourite teacher or preacher?
  *or*
- What does this passage say to me right now, in plain English?

The question which we *should* ask ourselves is:

● How did the original readers understand this?

This is a hard question to answer because it involves looking at the text in its original language, in the context of the whole book and in the context of its culture and history. Often it cannot be answered with certainty, but we do have to make an effort because this is the best chance we have for discovering what the author intended to communicate to his readers.

As Christians we have to assume that the Holy Spirit was able to convey truth accurately to the original readers in language and concepts which they would understand. We who come later have to do more work than they did in order to understand the same message, because we have to learn an ancient language and read it through the mindset of ancient thought-forms.

## Modern readers have to work harder

As 21st-century readers we will always be at a disadvantage because we are not native readers of ancient Greek or Hebrew, so we have to rely on scholars to translate the texts for us. Also we are not living in a Roman city or in ancient Jewish culture so we have to learn how they thought and wrote and lived before we can be sure that we understand the translated texts.

For example, when the Bible speaks about "the God who searches the kidneys and heart" (Jer. 20.12; Rev. 2.23),[26] it means that 'God knows our emotions and thoughts' because the ancients regarded the kidneys as the seat of emotions and the heart as the source of thoughts. If we did not understand these ancient concepts of human anatomy, these texts would give us a very strange idea about God's interest in our internal organs!

Another example is the story of Zacchaeus, where we can miss the whole point of the story in Luke 19 unless we have some background knowledge of ancient Jewish culture. We would not understand Jesus' love as expressed in this story unless we knew that tax collectors were the hated lackeys of the Roman occupation – something which we are *not* told in Scripture but learn from other historical sources. We would not understand the crowd's extreme consternation about Jesus eating with sinners unless we knew about the fanatical concern which most Jews had about purity laws – the details of which we only know from outside the New Testament. Zacchaeus kept much of his fortune, so Jesus told a parable about the wise use of money, but this parable makes no sense unless we know that ten *minas* (which older translations call "ten pounds") was a *huge* amount of money. None of this background knowledge is found in Scripture, but it is necessary for understanding Luke's message.

## Scripture alone is not always enough

Some would say that Scripture contains everything we need to know – a principle which is sometimes misleadingly called *Sola Scriptura* ('Scripture alone'). It is misleading because the real principle of *Sola Scriptura* is that everything which is *necessary for salvation* can be found by a plain reading of Scripture – as we see in the definition in the Westminster Confession:

> "The whole counsel of God, concerning all things necessary for his own glory, man's salvation, faith, and life, is either expressly set down in Scripture, or by good and necessary consequence may be deduced from Scripture... All things in Scripture are not alike plain in themselves, nor alike clear unto all, yet those things which are necessary to be known, believed, and observed, for salvation, are so clearly propounded and opened in some place of Scripture or other, that not only the learned, but the unlearned, in a due use of the ordinary means, may attain unto a sufficient understanding of them..."

Although divorce and remarriage are important topics, they are not necessary for salvation, and they do not therefore fall under the remit of *Sola Scriptura* as envisioned by the Reformers. As the Westminster Confession says, there are many doctrines (such as divorce and remarriage) which are "not plain in themselves, nor clear unto all".

We cannot approach Scripture without historic perspective. If we try to read it without taking into account how people thought at the time it was written, we will misunderstand a great deal of what God says to us. In this book we have often found that insights into ancient culture and language help us to understand what the Bible teaches about divorce and remarriage.

## An explosion of information

How much would you know about the two World Wars if you had never had access to any newspapers, books or films about them? Even if your parents or grandparents told you about the war, how much would you pass on to your children? Fortunately we do have detailed archives and yet some people are still able to convince themselves that the holocaust never happened. It seems paradoxical, but historians and archaeologists in the future will have a better chance of sorting out the truth than we do, when everything has been analysed carefully.

Similarly we have a better chance of understanding the New Testament in its original context than the 2nd-century Church Fathers. We have a greater knowledge of the language and culture of the 1st century than they did, partly because we can have a more accurate perspective on the changes that happened by looking at it from a distance. We also know more because we benefit from centuries of work by scholars of language and history and, although many important documents have been lost, we have better access to ancient sources than anyone living in the 2nd century.

A library of a hundred books would be a fabulous treasure for any ancient university, let alone an individual church scholar in the 2nd century. Most churches did not even own a complete Bible, while most scholars were not wealthy enough to own even one book of their own. Even the best scholars would be unlikely to see more than a couple of hundred books in their whole lifetime, and nowadays most ministers have more books than this in their personal library. Anyone with access to the World Wide Web can read virtually every ancient source and I carry a copy of most ancient literature around with me on my pocket computer. The Church Fathers could not even dream of such riches.

These texts have been analysed and re-analysed by scholars for hundreds of years, and although scholars are still making significant discoveries (as this book has shown), we now have a very clear idea of the language and culture of the 1st century.

## To conclude: Crossing the gulf

We have seen that there was a huge gulf between the language and culture of New Testament times and the 2nd-century Church Fathers, especially because of the destruction of Jerusalem and the complete change in Judaism at AD 70. Even without this type of cataclysm, we have seen that today we are separated from our own forefathers by changes in language and culture over as little as 25 years ago.

But it still seems strange that the early church itself did not notice that their teaching had changed, and it is equally strange that modern scholars have not pointed out this change before. These questions, which are potentially embarrassing to church theologians and scholars alike, are addressed in the next chapter.

**13**

# Conspiracy?

**Why has no-one explained all this before?**

Much of the information in this book has been available to scholars for more than a century, and you might well be asking why the church has not re-examined its teaching on divorce and remarriage to take it into account. Was it simply due to incompetence and the inability to fit all the facts together? Or was there a conspiracy? Although one of the Dead Sea Scrolls *was* suppressed and the status quo of the church is a powerful consideration, I don't think there was a conspiracy – but you may disagree when you find out some of the facts.

## Revealing the Dead Sea Scrolls

From the day they were discovered, to the day of their full publication, the Dead Sea Scrolls were surrounded by mystery and intrigue. The delay in publication, due to the length of time it took for scholars to complete the huge task of editing the documents, provoked rumours that they were being deliberately suppressed. One such rumour suggested that the Vatican wanted to hide heretical details about Jesus, and another one said that some Jewish scholars were trying to hide embarrassing discoveries.

When the original scrolls were eventually put on public display in the specially built Shrine of the Book in Jerusalem, there was great excitement and the press were out in force, expecting to report scandalous revelations. A friend of mine, who was working on one of the texts at that time, told me that there was a huge commotion in the Librarian's office where the journalists were asking questions, but none of them went to actually see any of the newly unveiled ancient documents. The scholars did not bother to attend either because they already knew what the journalists were about to find out... there *were* no 'suppressed' documents.

## A suppressed divorce document

So the conspiracy theories were proved to be baseless? Well, no – there was one exception. One of the Dead Sea Scrolls *was* deliberately concealed. It had been discovered, alongside other documents written in the early 2nd century, at Murabba'at, a little distance from the Qumran caves. Milik, who was one of the scholars responsible for publishing the Dead Sea Scrolls, edited and published the Murabba'at documents promptly, except for this particular one which he gave to another scholar, Jonas Greenfield. Greenfield put the document in a drawer, and although he mentioned it in a couple of lectures, he refused to make the text public.

After Greenfield's death the document passed to a student of his, Ada Yardeni. She edited and published it in 1995 without any translation and with a limited circulation. It soon became clear why Greenfield had kept it hidden – it was a Jewish divorce certificate written by a woman. Greenfield had been an expert on Jewish marriage law and, like many other Jews, he had believed that 1st and 2nd-century Judaism represented a golden age when the Rabbinic law was kept very faithfully – and Rabbinic law, of course, did not allow women to initiate a divorce. This document had therefore been just too embarrassing for him to publish.

After it was eventually published there was a heated scholarly squabble. Some scholars proposed changing a few characters in the text so that it would read as if it were a letter written by a woman, where she was simply *quoting* the words of a divorce certificate which had been written by her former husband. Other scholars maintained that the text should be translated as it was, but this was confusing because it then read as if part of it was written by a man and part of it by a woman. My article in *Harvard Theological Review* ended this part of the debate because I pointed out that if the document is simply translated literally, it is clearly a divorce certificate, written by a male scribe *on behalf* of a woman to her husband.

It is significant that the woman was not citing any particular fault by her husband and so she was not applying for a divorce on the Exodus 21.10 grounds of neglect. She appeared, instead, to be basing her divorce on 'Any Cause' even though this type of divorce was, strictly speaking, only available to men.

## Jewish divorce changed in the 2nd century

Greenfield had wanted to believe that in the 1st- and 2nd-centuries, Rabbinic Judaism was identical to that of later orthodox Judaism, whereas this document, written in the early 2nd-century, shows that on the contrary Judaism was very much in transition throughout this period, particularly with regard to divorce and remarriage. By the early 2nd-century, the 'Any Cause' divorce had taken over to such an extent that the Biblical divorces for neglect, which early 1st-century Judaism allowed women to initiate, had already been forgotten, even by Jewish scribes.

Perhaps my assessment of Greenfield's delay in publication is unfair, because he may have still been studying the document, but this incident highlights the fact that sometimes a key piece of knowledge can be withheld by someone in an effort to prevent a dearly-held belief being shown to be wrong. Both Judaism and the Christian church can be equally guilty of ignoring important findings in order to maintain the status quo.

In spite of the above, I think the major reason why the church has not collated all this information accurately is due to confusion rather than conspiracy, because changes in society during the life of the early church led it to emphasise a different message in Jesus' words.

## A world dominated by sex

By the 2nd century, the Roman world had become dominated by sex: husbands and wives both had homosexual and heterosexual lovers; prostitutes were not only accepted, but were a normal part of cultured life; at a meal, the host was expected to provide professional sexual entertainment, called the 'after dinners'; and extra-marital affairs were made easier by the widespread use of primitive, though effective, contraception (and, when this failed, the babies were killed). Sex had become cheapened as a commodity, and sexual immorality was such an all-pervasive vice that even marital sex became tainted. The sexual act became despised and feared by the church as a source of corruption and spiritual disease and the church ended up even being suspicious of conjugal relations within marriage.

Many religious groups reacted against this trend by taking up a directly opposite stance – that is, by preaching abstinence from all unnecessary sexual contact.

Some Jewish groups had already started to think this way in the 1st century. We know that the Dead Sea community kept sexual contact to a minimum and there were probably other smaller Jewish groups who did the same. Some of the Corinthian converts seem to have been influenced by this type of group because they asked Paul what he thought about the saying, "It is good for a man not to have sexual relations with a woman" (1 Cor. 7.1). Paul rejected this teaching on the standard Jewish grounds that sex was a good and necessary component of any marriage (vv. 2–5).

By the 2nd century many more Jews had become suspicious of sex. No pious Jew could actually reject sex completely – because having children was compulsory – but they could refrain from it after they had children. The only unmarried Rabbi we know of, R. Ben Assi, lived in the 2nd century. He *had* been married (so he had fulfilled his religious duty), but he refused to get remarried, even though everyone expected him to do so. He defended himself by saying that he was married to the Scriptures and was too busy. His potential father-in-law, Akiva, was probably sympathetic because although he was married, he had spent 14 years away from his wife in order to study at the Rabbinic academy in Jamnia.

These two 2nd-century Rabbis were members of an ascetic movement which avoided unnecessary sexual relations and other activities in pursuit of religious experiences by the means of meditation. Very few details about this movement survive because it was suppressed by mainstream Rabbis, but the evidence which we do have suggests that there was a strong underground movement within 2nd-century Judaism which tried to avoid sexual activity, despite the Jewish law that everyone should have children.

## Church fears about sex

The Christian church did not have a similar law about having children to give it a positive message about sex within marriage, so there was nothing to inhibit the ascetic movement. A large proportion of Christians started to assume that sex was evil or, at least, that it was a route towards evil and something to avoid, so although marriage was still celebrated, the avoidance of marriage was highly recommended. If a widow or widower remarried it was regarded as evidence of lasciviousness because they had already done their sexual duty by being married before; it was felt to be a wilful reversal of God's decision to end a period of sexual relations.

Tertullian was a Christian teacher at the end of the 2nd century who wrote books on the subject of marriage and open letters to his wife about remarriage, so we have a very detailed knowledge of what he believed on these subjects. He told his wife that she should not get remarried if he died because although this would not be sinful, it would not be God's will.

> When, through the will of God, the husband is deceased, the marriage likewise, by the will of God, deceases. Why should *you* restore what God has put an end to? ...For even if you do not "*sin*" in re-marrying, still he says "pressure of the flesh ensues." Wherefore, so far as we can, let us love the opport-unity of continence.[27]

The church gradually elevated celibacy higher and higher until, by the 9th century, the Roman church had decided that priests must be unmarried, that celibacy within marriage was a pious attitude, and that sexual relations without the goal of having children were sinful. This trend, which started in the 2nd century, was largely based on the misunderstanding that both Jesus and Paul taught that virginity was superior to the married state and that remarriage was always impious and often sinful.

## New teaching for a new age

In the context of this emphasis against sex, it was natural that the 2nd-century church would assume that Jesus taught remarriage was equivalent to sexual immorality and would not be surprised when he appeared to identify remarriage with "adultery". Even if the earliest of the Church Fathers had realised that their interpretation, or at least their emphasis of Jesus' words, was different from that of 1st-century believers, undoubtedly they would have considered their own teaching to be correct for their time.

What was more difficult to explain was why their teaching was so different from the Old Testament. They had to justify why Moses said that God allowed divorce and remarriage but Jesus seemed to condemn them both in the strongest language.

Most of the early Church Fathers explained it by simply saying that the Old Testament was for then and Jesus' teaching was for now. Others were uneasy with this explanation because it made God appear to have changed his mind and they tried to come up with other reasons. For example, Ptolemaeus (in the late 2nd century) said that Moses deliberately misrepresented God's commands, and Origen (in the early 3rd century) said that Moses simply made up the law about divorce to supply what was lacking in God's law. Despite their embarrassment, however, the Church Fathers were convinced that Jesus did reject the Old Testament laws.

## Tradition versus Scripture

In some branches of the Christian church one of the main ways of evaluating whether an interpretation of Scripture is correct is to measure it against the interpretations of the Church Fathers – though no-one would want to elevate the traditions of former church leaders above Scripture itself. But although it is certainly true that the commentaries of the Fathers are important for their insights and their knowledge of ancient traditions, this is not a guarantee that their interpretations are always correct.

In fact very few people today would defend some of the ways they interpreted Scripture. For example, almost all the early Church Fathers taught that there was no forgiveness for those who gave in to torture by pagan persecutors, and who cursed Christ to escape death. Since persecution was such a major problem for them we can understand *why* they interpreted texts such as Hebrews 10.26 in this way, but most people would now explain these texts as a condemnation of those who *wilfully* reject Christ, rather than those who break under torture.

## Disputes about doctrines

Arguments over doctrine have featured throughout the his-tory of the church. Early disputes included different interpretations about the Trinity and the Divinity of Christ, and conflicts over other things, such as the date of Easter and the status of the Holy Spirit resulted in the permanent division between the Eastern and Western Churches. Later disputes, including those over the authority of the Pope and other doctrines such as Indulgences (which were later changed during the Catholic church's own internal reformation), resulted in the Catholic/Protestant split. In more recent times, the church has been split over the status of scientific discoveries, the gifts of the Spirit, women's ministry and a host of other doctrines.

These conflicts have resulted in excommunication, torture, death and even wars. We might wish that the Holy Spirit would preserve us from such discord by making Scripture more plain, or by inspiring the scholars on both sides to agree with each other, but God does not work in this way. He gives us intelligence to think about difficult doctrines, and then expects us to listen to each other in humility and in a desire to find the truth. But human nature, being what it is, finds it difficult to review time-worn beliefs, even when new insights are clearly significant or when historical discoveries uncover information which has been lost.

## Discoveries ignored by theologians

Most of the historical data presented in this book has been known to Christian scholars for the last 150 years, but theologians have failed to apply it to the doctrine of marriage and divorce. Virtually every significant commentary on Matthew since 1850 mentions the dispute between the Hillelites and the Shammaites. Before then, the information had been available in the large volumes of Rabbinic law which were well known to Jews, though not to Christians.

Although the full significance of these Rabbinic texts was not clear until the discovery of the Dead Sea Scrolls and other documents from the Judaean desert, the clues were there and could have been correctly applied if there had been a willingness to look at the question dispassionately. Even Henry Alford, who wrote his *Greek Testament* commentary on Matthew in 1849, pointed out that Josephus divorced his wife on the grounds of 'Any Cause' and that Jesus took part in a debate between the Hillelites and Shammaites on this issue.[28]

There is actually a very good reason why the church has not reassessed its teaching about divorce and remarriage: church doctrine *should* not change. Preserving the status quo in this case *is* the best policy because God does not change and his truth does not change. Church doctrine should not be allowed to blow one way and then the other simply because society has changed. The purpose of this book has not been to argue for a new interpretation of Scripture but for an *old* one – i.e. the interpretation of the hearers and readers of the words of Jesus and Paul in the 1st century.

## To conclude: Reversing the change in church doctrine

It must be admitted that changes in society *have* been an incentive for this study. Although I've pursued the subject with the rigour and discipline of a scholar, my thoughts have often dwelt on actual abuse within Christian marriages and the misery which is produced by the church's teaching. I don't think that such abuse has increased in this generation, but the increasing openness of society means that we now hear much more about it, and church teaching has been brought into disrepute as a result.

Changes in society were also the incentive for the Church Fathers to accept a different interpretation of Jesus' teaching because they needed a way to turn the church away from the hedonistic world of the 2nd century. Like them, we are in danger of finding only what we *want* to find in the words of the New Testament, so we must make sure we listen to the Holy Spirit as well as to the scholars.

Jesus promised that the Holy Spirit would lead us into all truth, but this depends on our listening to him. We know that the Holy Spirit will not force us to hear the truth – because theologians and scholars have not preserved the church from divisions or even wars in the past – so must be willing to listen to each other and, most of all, to listen to Scripture. We should use our God-given intelligence while we seek to understand and apply his word and we should pray for God to point out the truth to us. And, of course, we should be prepared to admit that we might be wrong.

## Further Reading

### Dead Sea Scrolls and conspiracies

*The Library of Qumran* by Hartmut Stegemann (Eerdmans, 1998) is a good overview of the findings, and the conclusions which we can draw from them.

*Jesus, Qumran and the Vatican* by Otto Betz and Rainer Riesner (Crossroad, 1994) debunks the conspiracy theories once for all.

### The suppressed divorce certificate

My "Jewish Women Divorcing their Husbands in Early Judaism: The Background to Papyrus Se`elim 13" (*Harvard Theological Review* 92, 1999, 349–57) corrected previous translations which were based on an emended version of this contract and discus-ses the Jewish divorce laws of the 2nd-century.

Chapter 10 of *Integrating Women Into Second Temple History* by Tal Ilan (Hendrickson, 2001) gives a wider discussion of this document.

### 1st- and 2nd-century views on sex and feminism

"The 'New' Roman Wife and 1 Timothy 2.9–15: The search for a Sitz im Leben" by Bruce Winter (*Tyndale Bulletin* 51, 2000, 283–92) looks at feminism in the 1st century.

*Paul on marriage and celibacy: the Hellenistic background of 1 Corinthians 7* by Will Deming (Cambridge University Press, 1995) looks mainly at asceticism among Greek philosophers but also the early Church Fathers.

"Marriage, Divorce and Adultery" by Craig Keener in *Dictionary of Later New Testament & its Development* (InterVarsity Press 1997) traces the start of asceticism in the church to the Shepherd of Hermas in the second half of the 2nd-century, though Hermas is probably no more than the first enthusiastic exponent of it.

# 14

# What Should the Church Do Now?

### Biblical principles in practice

If you have come straight here without reading the previous chapters, please let me encourage you to go back and do so; otherwise you will find out the book's conclusions but you will not know about its Scriptural foundations. The purpose of this book has been to give you information that will help you to make up your own mind about the Bible's teaching and the purpose of this chapter is to remind you what we have found out so that we can put it together as a set of Biblical principles.

## Summary of this book

**Chapter 1** reviewed the church's traditional teaching on divorce and remarriage which many pastors have found to be unworkable. It also pointed out that sometimes what we *think* is in the Bible is not actually there.

**Chapter 2** showed us that God's ideal for marriage was for a loving, lifetime relationship and yet we also saw that the Old Testament is very practical with regard to the sin of marriage break-up. In the ancient Near East women could be abandoned by their husbands and then reclaimed by them in the future. This meant they were never free to find another husband to help bring up the children. God dealt with this problem in Israel by commanding that a husband who left his wife must give her a divorce certificate which gave her the right to remarry.

In **chapter 3** we found that God himself is a divorcee. The Old Testament prophets described God's relationship with Israel as if it was a marriage: when Israel worshipped other gods, she was likened to an unfaithful wife; she broke all her marriage vows while God continued to clothe, feed and love her faithfully. We saw that the prophets did not regard divorce itself as an evil act, but considered the breaking of marriage vows as the sin which broke up the marriage. God was the victim in his relationship with Israel and was therefore entitled to decide when the marriage was over. God's divorce also gave us an insight into the way he felt about divorce: he hates it because it means that promises in the marriage contract have been broken (Mal. 2.14–16).

**Chapter 4** reminded us that Jesus affirmed the teaching of the Old Testament – so we cannot simply reject the moral principles which we find there – and, in **chapter 5**, we saw that he criticised the Pharisees for abandoning Old Testament teaching when they introduced the new groundless type of divorce named 'Any Cause'. Jesus defended the plain meaning of the Old Testament phrase "a cause of sexual immorality" which he (and the Shammaites) said meant "nothing except 'Sexual Immorality'", i.e. adultery. Jesus also emphasised that divorce was never compulsory (even where adultery had taken place) and that believers should only divorce someone who was "hard-hearted" i.e. stubbornly unrepentant, like Israel was.

In **chapter 6** we saw that Paul was equally critical of groundless divorces. He told believers that they should not use the Roman divorce-by-separation and if they *had* separated they should try if possible to reconcile and remarry their partner. On the other hand, if someone had divorced *them*, Paul recognised that there wasn't anything they could do about it so in this case he said they were 'not enslaved' (which is what any divorce certificate would have told them). He accepted that being divorced against your will could be regarded as a valid Biblical divorce on the grounds of neglect.

Many people believe that marriage lasts till death, whether or not the the couple think they are divorced. **Chapter 7** looked at this point of view in the light of the Bible and found no basis for this interpretation. Many people also teach that a Christian should never divorce, even in cases of abuse, but **chapter 8** pointed out that the Old Testament law – which gave the neglected or abused partner the right to a divorce – was not repealed by Jesus and that Paul assumed that it still applied.

What about remarriage after divorce? The New Testament is remarkably vague on this important issue but **chapter 9** pointed out that 1st-century believers would have had no uncertainty because the right to remarry was taken for granted. It was a legal right which was recorded in all Jewish divorce certificates and in Roman law remarriage was actually a legal *duty*. Christians would no doubt have avoided remarriage if they had been told to, but they would have needed a very clear instruction because to do so would mean breaking the law. Neither Paul or Jesus gave this instruction, however, and although Paul never actually says "A divorcee may remarry", we saw that some of his teaching assumes that remarriage *is* allowed for Christians.

In **chapter 10** we looked at the difficult situation of those who have remarried after an invalid divorce. Jesus said this type of remarriage was like adultery, but we concluded that he did not want these couples to get divorced any more than he wanted us to treat a foul-tempered outburst as if it were literally murder or treat lustful thinking as though this was literally committing adultery. We also found that when Paul told abandoned believers that they could remarry because "God has called you to peace", he was using legal jargon which meant "this case is decided on pragmatic grounds". Even guilty partners can remarry because God is able to forgive someone who repents of an invalid divorce which cannot be reconciled without breaking up another marriage.

**Chapter 11** showed that our modern wedding service still retains the vows which originated from Exodus 21. We were able to trace the wording in the earliest English marriage  service back to both Jewish marriage contracts and Ephesians 5.28–29 where 'to love, honour and cherish' (and other variations) originate. I also shared my experience of using a service of repentance before remarrying divorcees.

Why was Jesus' teaching misunderstood so soon? **Chapter 12** showed that the destruction of the Temple in AD 70 marked a huge change in the culture and theology of Judaism as well as sealing the rift between Christians and Jews. This meant that Christians no longer understood the Rabbinic legal phrases which Jesus and Paul used like 'Any Cause' and 'God has called you to peace'.

**Chapter 13** asked why it has taken so long to realise that this misunderstanding had occurred and concluded that it is due to confusion rather than a conspiracy. The stand which the 2nd-century church took against sexual immorality made their new emphasis against remarriage (a misinterpretation of Jesus' teaching) seem normal. Once this new interpretation had become church doctrine it was difficult for the church to come to terms with the fact that a misunderstanding had taken place.

## Similar conclusions by the Reformers without the recent discoveries

This book has uncovered several pieces of information which are needed to help us understand what the Bible means:

- The need for a divorce certificate in Moses' law is explained by the fact that a husband in the ancient Near East had the right to reclaim a wife he had abandoned.

- The question which the Pharisees asked Jesus makes sense when we know about the new 'Any Cause' divorces at that time.

- Jesus' silence about the other Old Testament grounds for divorce is unsurprising when we find that all Jews in Jesus' day accepted their validity.
- Paul's teaching about 'separation' relates to the Roman practice of divorce-by-separation.

- The lack of clear teaching about remarriage in the New Testament has to be seen in the light of the legal right and duty to remarry that existed in the 1st century.

Although this new information is important for *demonstrating* what the text means we are still able to understand the text correctly without it. When the Reformers read the Bible, with relatively independent minds, they came to many of the same conclusions to which this new evidence leads us.

Erasmus realised that marriage was not a "sacrament" which continued till death despite divorce, and therefore he allowed remarriage after divorce for adultery or abandonment by an unbeliever. All the major Reformers agreed with his conclusions and Luther also allowed divorce for abandonment by a believer. Other Reformers, such as Zwingli and Bullinger, said that the New Testament did not list *all* the grounds for divorce so they could allow other grounds such as abuse. Cranmer wanted to base Anglican theology on his *Reformatio Legum Ecclesiasticarum* which allowed divorce and remarriage after adultery, desertion, prolonged absence, mortal hatred or cruelty, but this reform was prevented by Elizabeth I.

## Modern theologians with similar conclusions

Many modern theologians have come to similar conclusions to those in this book, though they have usually admitted that they did not have sufficient Biblical support for them. They have based their conclusions on the *principles* in the Bible rather than the details in these

difficult texts on divorce and remarriage. Some of the more successful attempts at Biblical exegesis have been:

> *To Have and To Hold: The Marriage Covenant and the Discipline of Divorce*
> (Collins, 1979) by David Atkinson, who has a very good understand-
> ing of Biblical marriage as a contract.

> *Divorce and Remarriage: Recovering the Biblical View* (Harper and Row,
> 1987) by William F. Luck, who recognised the importance of Exodus
> 21.10–11 but failed to follow this text into the New Testament.

> *...And Marries Another: Divorce and Remarriage in the Teaching of the New
> Testament* (Hendrickson, 1991) by Craig S. Keener, who recognised Paul's
> references to the Roman divorce-by-separation and pointed out most of
> the Jewish background to the Gospel accounts.

> *No Way Out? – Pastoral Care of the Divorced and Remarried* (St Paul
> Publications, 1989) by Bernard Haring, a Catholic priest and lecturer in
> Moral Theology, who wrote this very honest book while dying of can-
> cer. He commended the Greek Orthodox theology of allowing divorce
> and remarriage after a *marriage* has died rather than waiting for a for-
> mer partner to die.

Most pastoral theologians have concluded on pragmatic grounds that we
must allow divorce for abandonment and cruelty, and most also include
emotional and material neglect as valid grounds for divorce. They also
point out that it is unjust to punish an innocent partner in the same way
as a partner who broke up a marriage by preventing both of them from
remarrying until their partner dies. Most of them would add that even
the guilty partner should be allowed to remarry after repentance because
the church would otherwise have to decide who is 'innocent'. It would
also be making marriage break-up into an unforgivable sin.

## Biblical principles and church policy

These conclusions by pastoral theologians, which until now were not
often based on Scripture, are very similar to the principles which we
have discovered in the Bible:

1. Marriage is a lifetime contract between two partners and marriage
   vows are the stipulations of this contract.

2. Both partners vow to provide material support and physical affection and to be sexually faithful to each other.

3. If one partner breaks a marriage vow the other has the right to decide either to end the marriage with a divorce or to carry on.

4. Divorce should only take place if vows have been broken and it is always sinful to break these vows.

5. Jesus added the caveat that we should forgive an erring partner unless they break their vows continuously or without repentance.

6. Paul added the caveat that if a divorce takes place without citing broken vows, remarriage is only allowed if reconciliation is impossible.

The over-riding principle in all these is that the wronged partner must be able to choose – they must be able to decide whether to regard the marriage contract as broken or whether to persevere with it, and if they have been divorced against their will in a civil court, they should be able to decide whether to attempt a reconciliation.

On the basis of these principles a church might adopt the following set of policies:

1. The Biblical grounds for divorce are adultery, neglect or abuse, which is equivalent to broken marriage vows.

2. No-one should initiate a divorce unless their partner is guilty of repeatedly or unrepentantly breaking their marriage vows.

3. No-one should separate from their marriage partner without intending to divorce them.

4. If someone has divorced or separated without Biblical grounds, they should attempt a reconciliation with their former partner.

5. Remarriage is allowed in church for any divorcee after a service of repentance, unless they have divorced an innocent partner who wants to be reconciled.

## Contradictions in present church policy

Most churches have contradictions in their policies with regard to divorce because they allow divorce for adultery but not for attempted murder. And when they *do* allow divorce this is actually no more than separation, because they do not allow remarriage. This is contrary to Paul's teaching that those who are married should live together and care for each other (1 Cor. 7.3–5, 33–34). In effect, this teaching has invented a new state somewhere between married and single which Augustine named "separation from house and hearth" (*a mensa et thoro*). Although the majority of the Reformers rejected this concept, most Protestant churches implicitly accept it when they allow someone to separate from a partner without divorcing them.

This new concept of 'separation' without divorce results in a situation where people are forced to live singly without being able to remarry. This brings us, full circle, back to the situation that existed before the Law of Moses, where a husband could abandon a wife without giving her the freedom to remarry – a situation which God remedied by commanding that the woman should be given a divorce certificate.

Among all the hundreds of different combinations of possible ways to interpret the Biblical teaching on divorce and remarriage I have found only two which are fully coherent without any internal contradictions and which can be said to be based on Scripture. The first says that the New Testament does not allow divorce at all because marriage lasts till death and Jesus and Paul only allowed exceptions to this rule because they were necessitated by Jewish and Graeco-Roman law. The reason for Jesus allowing divorce after adultery was because it was compulsory for the Jews to divorce after a wife's adultery. Likewise, Paul made an exception in the case of separation by an unbeliever, because the Graeco-Roman world regarded separation as divorce. When this teaching is applied to our society it means that a believer should never divorce and, if they are divorced against their will, they cannot remarry.

This view is best represented by Heth & Wenham in *Jesus and Divorce* (though they do not include the explanation for Paul's exception). It is based on the assumption that Jewish believers could be forced to divorce adulterous partners but this is erroneous because there was no ruling body with the power to enforce such a command. Jewish society had many religious authorities (Pharisee, Sadducee, Essene etc.) but none of them could impose their will – except by excommunicating someone from their own synagogue.

The only other coherent solution is the one which 1st-century believers would have inferred from the New Testament – that divorce is only allowed for the victim of broken marriage vows and that the right to remarriage is implicit in any divorce. In our society this would mean that a believer should only divorce if they have Biblical grounds (even if these ground are not named as the legal basis for their divorce) and that all divorcees may remarry unless their innocent ex-partner wants a reconciliation.

## How can we apply these findings?

What can we do with the results of this study? In many churches, where tradition is strongest, the answer will be – very little. The ship of the church is too large and its canon law is too well established for it to change course now, even if a huge number of people are leaning on the rudder. Smaller, younger denominations have a better chance to change direction and to return to a 1st-century interpretation of the Bible.

Re-asserting these principles is made possible by the remarkable fact that the Holy Spirit has preserved the Biblical marriage vows in the wedding services of virtually every Christian denomination. It is amazing that despite all the changes in church theology with regard to marriage and divorce, the wording of our wedding services has remained fairly constant, so that church practice has continued to be centred on the original Biblical marriage vows. When we marry we all still promise to love, nourish, cherish and be faithful to each other. Although the exact wording varies in different marriage services (as it did in New Testament times) the principles of the Biblical marriage have remained intact. This makes it much easier to re-introduce the concept of divorce based on broken marriage vows because all Christian marriages are already based on these Biblical vows.

Individual churches will approach this in different ways. Some will merely teach their flock that this is what believers *should* do, while others will attempt to back it up with some kind of church discipline such as excommunication or temporary exclusion from Communion, or by refusing to remarry those who divorce their partners without Biblical grounds. I'd like to think that churches will concentrate less on discipline and more on pastoral counselling.

Marriage counselling is often hampered by the lack of a coherent Biblical approach to divorce and remarriage. In the light of this study a Christian counsellor can say with confidence that a believer does have grounds for divorce in cases of adultery, abuse or neglect but that Jesus asked us to forgive a partner who repents after breaking their vows. Jesus allowed us to divorce a 'hard-hearted' partner, but neither he nor Paul chose to define how much neglect was too much – unlike the Rabbis who defined the minimum amount of food, clothing and conjugal love that was due.

This Biblical teaching gives a person who is suffering within a marriage both an encouragement to persevere and a safety net when they find they cannot cope with it any more. They can, if necessary, divorce their 'hard-hearted' partner in the know-ledge that God himself was forced down this route when Israel hard-heartedly broke her marriage vows to him. The divorce which God went through brought much pain and suffering, according to the prophets, and no-one expects divorce to bring happiness, but sometimes divorce is necessary in order to end the sinfulness of repeated and unrepentant breaking of marriage vows. Divorce is never 'good' but sometimes it is the only way to end the 'evil' of a broken marriage.

## To conclude: Principles for real life

We can now understand what Jesus and Paul were saying to their listeners about divorce and remarriage, which means that we can now understand what God is saying to us. We have found that the New Testament teaching is both practical and caring. God's love reaches out to those who are struggling in a broken marriage, to the innocent divorcee, and also to the sinner who has broken their marriage vows and repented.

We have found a set of Biblical principles which some denominations will be able to apply in their church practice and which all churches will find useful in marriage counselling. Applying these principles will not always be easy because principles are not the same as rules and no two marriages are the same. Some of the practical problems which arise are illustrated by the real-life situations in the next chapter.

## Further Reading

### *Teaching of the Reformers*

The second half of chapter 9 "History of Divorce" in my *Divorce and Remarriage in the Bible* (Eerdmans, 2002) examines the different teachings of the Reformers, especially Erasmus and Luther.

"Divorce and Remarriage from the Early Church to John Wesley" by David L. Smith (*Trinity Journal*, 11 NS, 1990, 131–142) covers more Reformers including Calvin, Tyndale and Cranmer.

### Biblical basis for divorce for abuse

Chapter 10 "Modern Re-interpretations" in my *Divorce and Remarriage in the Bible* (Eerdmans, 2002) examines the multitude of different ways in which the Biblical texts have been interpreted.

*Marriage, Divorce & Remarriage in the Bible* by Jay Adams (Presbyterian and Reformed Publishing Co, 1980) argues for divorce for abandonment by believers because they are acting like non-believers.

*Putting Asunder: Divorce and Remarriage in Biblical and pastoral perspective* by Stephen Clark (Brynterion Press, 1999) argues that believers who act against the interest of the marriage can be divorced because they act like non-believers who don't want the marriage to continue (as in 1 Cor. 7.12–13).

# 15

# Dear Pastor...

**Real-life problems from my mailbox**

I have a parish of hundreds of thousands through a very busy website (www.Instone-Brewer.com). I put most of my work on the site as I write it; about a thousand people visit it per week and a few of them email me. This came yesterday from an American man:

> When I found your website I cried (for joy) and I just wanted to thank you. I was in a church that taught there was no reason to get divorced, except perhaps adultery. In my marriage, I was in a pervasive emotionally-abusive situation and the counsel of my Christian friends was to "hang in there". Finally, I had a dream where I was standing before God and I had done something violent to end the abuse. God asked me a question: "Why did you not just leave?" It was then that I knew I needed to get out of my marriage, regardless of what my church taught and what my friends said. They all asked me what was the Biblical basis of my divorce, as I was abused but they did not see that as a valid reason...

> I can now point them to your website for a scholarly and very credible explanation of my position. As you say, the whole position on marriage and divorce is made coherent by understanding the Jewish context. I ordered 3 copies of your book, one for me, one for my pastor, and one for my psychological counselor. I thank God that you have had the courage to speak the truth in love as you understand it. Praise God!

A British woman emailed me a few weeks ago:

> Just came across your web pages completely by accident whilst researching into the effects of divorce on pensions!! As a Christian and

an active member of a parochial church council (PCC), my decision to divorce my abusive husband after six and a half years was not taken lightly and only after years of soul searching, prayer and finally desperation as I clambered back from depression and breakdown. I knew that God did not intend for me to suffer as I was suffering yet could find no other answer. I concluded that the Biblical ideal of marriage could only be attained if both parties were aiming for the same goal and could not believe that I was expected to continue living in this manner despite evidence to the contrary. A few months prior to making my decision, I consulted my parish rector and discussed my anguish at length and he did persuade me to try to make it work.

Following my decision, I sent a letter of resignation to the PCC explaining that due to my situation, I no longer felt it appropriate to continue serving on the council and that I was having problems dealing with the compromisation of my faith. I received a letter thanking me for my work over the years and wishing me luck in the future. No member of my church has contacted me since, leaving me with an even greater feeling of failure and sin. I have felt unable to walk into my church since and have not done so.

## The theory is good, but does it work?

I have heard many stories like these where divorcees have felt let down by their church just when they need its help most. A huge number of people are hurt and harmed during the course of their marriage but we will never know exactly how many because often they suffer in secret. In the past, women were the victims of broken marriage vows more often than men, but things are now equalising. Both men and women commit adultery, and both men and women are abusive or neglectful, though men are much more likely to be violent.

The teaching of the church has compounded much of this hurt rather than alleviating it. Victims of continuing abuse have been told that they must stay married and, even if they do get divorced, they have been told that they cannot remarry until their former partner has died. And sometimes those who have divorced and remarried are told by their church that they must now divorce their new spouse because, in God's eyes, they are still married to the person who abused or neglected them – so the church makes them a victim for a second time.

Most of my work on divorce and remarriage was done after I left the church pastorate to become a Research Fellow of an academic institution. While my mind wandered freely among the academic towers of Cambridge, my feet were kept firmly on the ground by a wide circle of church contacts and by emails like those in this chapter. The questions people asked often forced me to face up to practical implications of my studies which I had not considered. These emails became, for me, a test by which my work could be judged, because if my interpretation of Scripture is correct, I would also expect it to be practical in pastoral situations. Whether or not my work has passed this test is for you to judge as you read these emails over my shoulder and see my replies.

## Email from a woman who stayed with her abusive husband

It has always been more important to me not to sin than to accommodate happiness in my life. Well, not always, or else I wouldn't have ended up in this situation in the first place, but it did at least become the most important eventually. Because of that, I wouldn't divorce. But this stance left me with an even bigger problem. My husband learned that he could do just about anything and I would take it because of my beliefs, and he did. All the way from beatings to going just to the line and stopping in other activities. He's entertained thoughts of at least three girls; dated one... and let me know it was happening. I think my parents concluded that I was probably dropped on my head when I was little... why else would I be so... stupid! ...to stay with a man who did these things.

I must tell you... your work on divorce and remarriage has got to be the best I've ever seen, and I've read a lot. Your writings aren't unusual in the position you take as much as many have offered a similar perspective, but it's almost always based on..."God doesn't want you to suffer" or..."common sense says". It seemed to me that was really only looking for loopholes in God's word. But, the more I read in your writings, the more I realized that because we don't understand this issue many people sincerely wanting to follow God have ended up in bondage to their own good intentions. Your writings are remarkable. Its going to take me a little time to reposition myself from my old ways of thinking, but... I'm very grateful to you for presenting a truly Biblical perspective on this issue, that is based on solid objective truth and not an emotional plea for "there must be some way out". God's blessings.

**Reply:** I'm so pleased that you wanted to follow Jesus' command, even when it is difficult. As you realise, I've concluded that the church has made things much more difficult for you than they need be. God loves you, and knows that you are a victim, as well as knowing the ways in which you may perhaps have contributed to this breakdown. You are right that some Bible teachers appear to be looking for loopholes in the Bible's teaching – to find a "fair" solution – but please don't look down on them for doing this. They are trying to find a way to hold on to God's Word at the same time as holding on to the fact of God's love. I am fortunate to have found the 'key' to understanding these texts, but good theologians, like Luther, have instinctively come to the same conclusions without being able to justify them fully.

God be with you as you seek his will at this time.

## Email from a woman in a loveless marriage

I have a question on my divorce and would like to know the Biblical stand point on it being a born again Christian (albeit back slidden).

When you say "They affirmed the ground for divorce in Deuteronomy 24:1 (adultery) and the other grounds for divorce in Exodus 21:10f (neglect of material support and physical affection)" can I assume that the neglect of physical affection can also mean non-regular consummation of that marriage? I have been torturing myself for ages that I had no right to seek a divorce despite 10 years of virtually total 'neglect' in our marriage. By the age of 31 I felt I had given him enough time and chance to try and do something about it.

**Reply:** This issue is one of the most difficult things about the passage in Exodus 21.10f because there are so many possible reasons for refusing conjugal activity within marriage. When passions cool, the act of love can become boring or even disgusting for some people, and who can allocate blame for lack of libido? Physical frailty creeps up unequally sometimes, leaving one partner wanting no more than a cuddle while leaving the other one frustrated. Sometimes medical and emotional problems intervene. Frequently these problems can be sorted out by talking them through – though I realise that it's hard to discuss these things – and often a counsellor is helpful. The Bible speaks in plain language on these issues and Paul is quite blunt! – so we should not treat sexual problems as unimportant or unspiritual.

Without knowing you and your former husband personally, it is impossible to know if you can divorce him for neglect of physical affection, and even if I did know you these things are not open to public scrutiny! It certainly sounds from what you say that your husband was not honouring his debt of love (as Paul puts it in 1 Cor. 7.3–5) and it sounds as though you gave him many opportunities to change his ways. If you honestly conclude that your husband *has* unjustifiably denied you your right to sexual relations and refuses to change, then it sounds as though you do have Biblical grounds for divorce – but only you and God know.

## Email about a foolish marriage

> My daughter married a man that she did not love. She is not sure why she married him other than she was in love with the idea of the wedding. She has stayed married for four years and love for him has never grown. She is miserable and her unhappiness is wearing heavy on her emotional and physical health. She needs spiritual direction. Could you please help.

**Reply:** This is a very sad situation but I can't see that there is any Biblical 'way out' for her because the promises which your daughter made are valid, even if they were made unthinkingly or for foolish reasons. Catholic theologians might allow annulment of a marriage in this situation – i.e. they would declare that the marriage never started because the vows were taken in an invalid way, without sufficient forethought. A Catholic court would certainly annul a marriage if one of the couple felt that they were under emotional duress from their parents or if they were not sufficiently mature when they made their vows. Personally I don't like the idea of annulling a marriage. I think it's the responsibility of the minister who officiates at the wedding to make sure beforehand that the couple are properly prepared for their vows and to refuse to marry them if he thinks that they aren't.

The only Biblical grounds for divorce occur when one of the four marriage vows are broken and although some people might argue that the vow about 'conjugal love' means 'being in love', this is very unlikely. Equally someone might argue that the principle behind this, which we have termed 'physical affection', includes showing the natural affection which only comes from being 'in love'. However, this would be stretching the principle too far, because no-one can be *required* to be responsible for something which they cannot control.

Jesus discouraged divorce even when vows were clearly broken, saying that Moses did not 'command' divorce but he 'allowed' it when vows were broken in a 'hard-hearted' way, which means something like 'constantly' or 'unrepentantly'. Marriage is not just a convenient way for two people to live together – it is a sworn agreement which two people make to each other in God's presence that they will live for each other, come what may.

Love doesn't just come from 'chemistry' or from Cupid's arrow, but from human actions and reactions, from devotion and demonstrations of affection. Most marriages go through tough times when a couple fall 'out of love' but unless one of them has done something terrible there is usually no reason why this shouldn't be reversed. Arranged marriages, as in New Testament times, often start out with nothing more than one or two meetings during which the couple find that they like each other and agree to get married. Love can grow and it can re-grow, if both parties are willing to help it happen.

I realise that this is not the answer you may have wished to hear, and that there will be hard times ahead, but I pray that you will be able to help your daughter and son-in-law through this difficulty in their marriage.

## Email suggesting a solution: Jesus was only speaking about betrothal

I would like to thank you for your work in regards to the issue of Biblical divorce. Here in the States, many pastors refuse any type of divorce on the grounds that when Jesus was discoursing with the Pharisees, Jewish law only allowed divorce during the betrothal or one year period before the actual marriage. When Jesus made his fornication or *porneia* exception, their claim is that he was referring to the one year period before marriage. Essentially, they only allowed what we would in modern times call "broken engagements".

**Reply:** It's true that there was often a one-year betrothal in 1st-century Judaism and that the breaking of a betrothal required a divorce certificate. This certificate wasn't strictly necessary, but was given 'just in case', to provide proof that the bride was free to marry someone else. It's also true that if a person was unfaithful during the betrothal period it was considered equivalent to adultery. But, to answer your question, it is *not* true that divorce was only allowed during betrothal – the Pharisees allowed it at any point in marriage. And it is also not true that *porneia* (the Greek word for 'sexual immorality' in Mt. 19.9) only meant unfaithfulness during betrothal – it was a word with a wide meaning, including committing adultery, going to prostitutes (as in 1 Cor. 6.13–18), and all other forms of sexual immorality.

For this theory to work it would mean that Jesus used language differently from all the other Jews and Greeks of his time, so that when he used the word *porneia* he meant 'unfaithfulness during betrothal' instead of just 'sexual immorality' (the normal meaning of the word). If we believe that Jesus was honestly trying to communicate with his hearers (and readers) we have to assume that he meant what they would have thought he meant.

## Email from a guilty and repentant church leader

I am indeed an adulterer. I was a deacon in my church and an educator in school. However my wife and I were not a good match. None the less I stayed for 26 years. Tried hard to be dogmatic like her and her family. No dancing, no shorts, no public swimming, etc. Our marriage looked good on surface. No alcohol, no abuse, no gambling, etc. Great children.

When our oldest son was killed in a car accident, I lost it. I went on the road as an entertainer and went wild. No mistake. Just plain lust, low character, etc. We divorced. I apologised publicly in two churches, resigned as a deacon. Left our church. After two years I met a lady, and we have been dating several months now. She knows all my story and the shame and guilt I bear. The brand I carry. We started going to church in my hometown. I baptised her 5 months ago. The church loved it. But now if we marry the elders are going to admonish us and tell her she is living in adultery even though she had nothing to do with it. If we marry we will not be welcome any more and may be asked to leave since we will be living in public sin and are going to hell. Your comments please. How do I fight this?

**Reply:** What a sad story. No-one could fail to understand the strain you were under when your son was killed or to realise that your sin was partially caused by those circumstances. This doesn't mean that you did not sin – and you haven't tried to deny it. You have admitted your sin before God and the church, and like all confessed and repented sins, it is now forgiven.

Although the sin is forgiven, its consequences are still there – the promises which you made to your former wife remain broken and your children are still without their father. Paul said that in a situation like yours, i.e. if you divorced without Biblical grounds, you must remain unmarried while you seek reconciliation with your former partner. This means that before you remarry, you must make sure that your former wife does not want to be reconciled. You are the one who broke the marriage vows and she, as the wronged partner, should decide if she wants a reconciliation – though, of course, if she has remarried, then that marriage should not be broken up.

If your former wife does not want a reconciliation are you now free to remarry? On the basis of my research I would say, Yes. But, as you realise, many churches do not understand the Bible in this way, and I'm afraid you are probably right to expect problems. God be with you on the difficult road ahead.

## Email from a remarried man whose church wants him to get divorced

> My wife and I are both divorced. Her ex-husband is still alive, however, my ex-wife has passed away. We are very concerned about the issue of whether or not we are living in adultery, as it seems Jesus teaches. I have read some of your articles, and it appears that what is important is the REASON for the divorces. I know members of the Church of Christ that insist that the only way for us to escape living in adultery is to divorce one another and remain unmarried. I realise divorce is a travesty, it hurts children, parents, friends and many others. Please help us understand the truth. If we are in fact living in adultery, then I know there will never be any hope for us in serving the Lord – teaching, witnessing, or even attending our local church.
>
> Does our divorce and remarriage put us in a class of "unforgivable" people, if we insist on remaining married? That would appear to be the case. I can't honestly see how another divorce could make things right. I understand that you may not be able to answer this, as you probably are inundated with emails, as most of us are. However, I need an answer. Not smooth, easy words, but the truth.

**Reply:** I agree that another divorce won't help because two wrongs don't make a right. I also agree that Jesus' teaching about divorce does depend on the reason for the divorce – because he was criticising the new groundless divorce for 'Any Cause'.

Was your wife's divorce based on valid Biblical grounds? A Biblical divorce is one which is initiated by the victim of unfaithfulness, or of neglect of material support or physical affection, or of abuse. If it wasn't, then your church is right – technically you are committing adultery because your wife does not have a Biblically valid divorce.

If you are committing technical adultery Jesus did not mean that you should now divorce, any more than he expected that those who commit technical adultery by looking lustfully at someone should "gouge out their eyes". When he said to "gouge out your eye" and "cut off your hand and throw it away" (Mt. 5.29–30) he was using preacher's rhetoric to emphasise his point. And when Jesus said in the next verse that remarriage after an invalid divorce is technically adultery (Mt. 5.31–32), he was careful *not* to add, 'therefore divorce her' just in case someone foolishly acted on it! Unfortunately some people *did* castrate themselves based on what Jesus said and some people *do* teach 'therefore divorce' based on something Jesus *never* said.

I'm glad that you want to do the 'right' thing. I pray that God will guide you to the correct path.

## Email from someone who wants a service of repentance when she marries

> I came across your web site by chance, as if God was guiding me to your words. I have not found much consolation from the words of Christians (about remarriage).

> I am a Christian and have been a single parent for 6 years, my children are now teenagers, and I have been divorced for 5 years. I have now met someone who was divorced 20 years ago. Both divorces were based on a breakdown of the marriage and there was no third party involved. He was a Christian, but the breakdown of the marriage and subsequent divorce left him disillusioned with his Christian beliefs. So much so that one of his relations did not communicate with him for 12 years. He subsequently lived with a woman and her child for 15 years supporting both families, although never remarrying. We have a lot of

common interests, although he still turns his back on Christianity. In your paper you quote that you conduct a short service of 'repentance for broken promises', I have never heard of a service like this, although I feel that I would like something like that if I was ever to remarry.

However, how does this man get over the past and accept God's word again? Our relationship is developing through ploughing through arguing based on his nonacceptance to my Faith. I have told him that I don't see the need to place the difference in views between us. He is knowledgeable of why Christians take Communion, so I take it that he was a practising Christian before his divorce.

**Reply:** The happiness you've found seems fragile because your friend has rejected the faith which is so important to you. It might be that he has rejected the church because the church and Christians rejected him. When the question of marriage comes up this might prompt him to reconsider his faith, and a Service of Repentance may be just what he needs. When he sees that Jesus loves him and forgives his broken marriage, just as he forgives other broken promises, this may give him the courage to face Christians again. I pray that God may help you in your relationship with him.

## Email about some new Christians whom the church refused to marry

My wife & I were following up a young couple in our church (the husband had just trusted Christ on their first visit to our church) who were not married but were living together. Needless to say, it was a touchy situation, and we decided to focus on their spiritual growth & pray that the Holy Spirit would bring their need to change their living situation to their attention. Eventually we did speak to them about this, and they responded very well. They soon made plans to get married, and decided to stop living together until this happened.

However, she called our pastor after going to our church for over 6 months asking about getting married in our church and by him... At this point some of the church's "policies" had to be dealt with, and our pastor & I got together and visited this couple together. At that time he handed her the church policy re. marriage in our sanctuary and by the pastor. I watched as tears ran down her cheeks as she read this document. They almost left the church as a result of the hypocrisy in our policy, and it was only because of some close relationships developed, including that with my wife and I, that they have stayed and become very active. He now sings as part of our worship team and she is the church secretary.

Partially due to this and similar incidents, our church has changed our policy, and we have some spelled out conditions which are much more reasonable as well as have provided the opportunity to come before the elder board to talk about it. Our church policy now is that we will marry those for whom there no longer is a possibility of being reconciled to their former spouse, i.e. he/she has passed away or has remarried. That still does not cover all eventualities, such as when your former spouse is "living in sin" rather than choosing to remarry. Of course the church would rather error on the side of being conservative.

I am looking forward to the completion of your book. I may not agree with all of your arguments or conclusions, but I am sure it will help me to form a better understanding of what God has to say on this topic. I may recommend it to our elder board for reading, and suggest it to our pastor.

**Reply:** I'm really impressed by your church board which was willing to reconsider and change their policy in the light of this incident. It's too easy to dig your heels in and say: "We've always done it this way." But I also understand those who might want to stick with the church's traditional policies (even though they are harsh and seemingly hypocritical) because they believe them to be Biblical. We should always follow the Bible, even when it seems difficult. The amazing thing is that your new church policy is almost exactly what the Bible *does* say, according to my studies.

I pray that other churches will be like yours – ready to seek the Lord's will and ready to take into account the latest discoveries which help us understand the Bible's teaching.

## Email from someone who admits being judgmental

About 6 months ago I discovered that the wonderful person that I was dating (at that stage for 1.5 yrs) had been pre- viously married, and was divorced. I had known that he had a secret from his past and it had taken me months to convince him that I would not judge his past, because who he was now was important. Anyway, when he told me that he was divorced, I instantly thought that I had to end the relationship (hmmm so much for being non-judgmental). At the time I also saw the irony in that he could have done absolutely anything else (e.g. murder) and I could be with him, just not have been divorced.

Needless to say I did a lot of reading, and it is sites like yours which can make a difference to people's lives. So all I wanted to say was thankyou!!!

**Reply:** I'm really pleased that you were able to see past your prejudice. Some church boards make the mistake which you avoided. They would happily have an ex-murderer as their pastor, and even boast about it, but they would not want a divorcee, even if they were the innocent partner in the marriage break-up. It's a funny world.

## Email about a church where divorcees cannot be deacons

The deacons and pastor at my home church (Southern Baptist) have recently decided that members who have separated from their spouses (regardless of the length of the separation or whether there are Biblical grounds for divorce) cannot serve the church as deacons or on the church council.

They point to the qualification that leaders must be "good managers of their household" and that 1 Corinthians 7:10ff specifically prohibits marital separation. They also believe that divorced members have "resolved" their marital problems and, therefore, ARE eligible to serve in these capacities.

**Reply:** This is an interesting idea and I think it has a lot of good sense. I'm pleased to hear that your church isn't making the common mistake of interpreting "husband of one wife" (or literally "man of one woman" – 1 Tim. 3.2) and "wife of one husband" (or literally "woman of one man" – 1 Tim. 5.9) to mean 'not remarried'. In New Testament times those phrases meant "a one-woman man" or a "one-man woman" i.e. someone who was faithful.[29] Timothy was being told to make sure his deacons were not sexually immoral, which was very difficult in a society where you were allowed to sleep with your slaves and where a host was expected to provide prostitutes after a banquet.

I'm also pleased that your church is taking seriously Paul's teaching about separation, which most Christians treat far too lightly. Paul tells

Christians that they should not separate, except by agreement for a short period of prayer (1 Cor. 7.5). If you separate without divorcing, your partner is left in limbo and powerless. They are not able to have their old relationship with you and they can't move forward to form a new relationship. That's why Paul tells those who have separated that they must seek reconciliation (v. 11) and tells those who have been divorced by separation against their will that they are 'not enslaved' (v. 15) – i.e. they can treat the separation like a proper divorce which frees them to get remarried. Christians often think that separation is better than divorce – the opposite of what Paul taught. So, all in all, I think your church has got it about right.

## Email from Mozambique about polygamy and divorce-by-separation

We work in Beira, Mozambique where marriages form by coming together and end by separation. Faithfulness is uncommon and life long union rare. The people with whom we work are also polygamous. Our next door neighbour has three wives and 14 children. They frequently rely on the Old Testament to justify their way of life.

**Reply:** In the New Testament Jesus taught against polygamy (which was allowed in the Old Testament and still allowed in 1st-century Judaism) while Paul taught against divorce-by-separation (which was the normal way to get divorced in Graeco-Roman society) and against marital faithlessness (which was common in the Gentile world). It sounds like you are having to deal with the problems of all of these New Testament societies rolled into one!

We often ignore Jesus' teaching against polygamy – because most of us never face the issue – but it was an important part of his teaching in which he disagreed with the majority of Jews of his day. It must be exciting to see a situation where the New Testament applies so obviously but it must also be very difficult because you face the same overwhelming task as the early Christians. I pray that God will help you as he helped them.

## Email from someone who wants to know my motives

I appreciate the work you've done and I agree with the position you've taken.

Do you come from a broken home? Did your parent remarry? Have you been involved in a divorce? Have you been remarried?

Thank you again for your insightful work.

**Reply:** I'm extremely fortunate that no-one in my family is divorced. My mother married my father after the death of her first husband and I, my brother and two sisters are all once-married and remain happily married. But as a minister I met many Christians whose marriages have broken up and whose remarriages appear to be blessed by God. It is for them that I carried out these studies and for those in destructive marriages who feel that they are not allowed to divorce. Also, I would be pleased if those who will be getting married, and those who are already married, would pay careful attention to the Bible's emphasis on marriage vows. We often take these vows too lightly.

## Email from someone who thinks I am teaching this for money

A broad path to hell and a narrow one to heaven. All the excuses for divorce and remarriage the preachers come up with to keep their money coming in. GOD doesn't change; men do. You can't break a covenant that both of you make to GOD and GOD seals it when you marry. The one that commits adultery and remarries is committing adultery and should get divorced. But I understand you need your income and tithe money. You know it is amazing to me, they go uptown to get married and downtown to get divorced or to a money hungry so called preacher to tell them its alright. A good preacher would say no divorce and if you do, you have to live a single life the rest of your life because that's what you reap of your sowing.

The only way to stop an adulterous marriage is to get out of it. He told the woman at the well "Go and sin no more" – no more sex or men. Too bad if they have to raise their kids by themselves; they reap what they sow. I am not trying to be hard on people but other people reaped what they sowed in the Bible. Like Moses for getting upset and hitting a rock – sounds petty to me, but not to GOD. It's amazing how preachers can bend the truth and twist it to fit their wants and desires. But GOD said they would in the last day.

**Reply:** I sympathise with your criticism of preachers who teach what people want to hear in order to gain a larger income, though this is very rare. I have applied all the knowledge and intelligence which the Lord has given me to studying the Bible and I ask you to prayerfully judge what I have found out, instead of rejecting it merely because the conclusions are different from what you think the Bible says.

Although I'm not teaching these things in order to make money, I do hope that you will buy my book!

## It is for you to judge

These emails demonstrate that there are a lot of people who need practical solutions and I hope I've been able to show you that the Bible does have them. Most of the work behind these studies was conducted in the privileged academic environs of Cambridge, using the unparalleled resources of the Tyndale House library. Here I had access to a vast array of historical sources, including all the relevant ancient Jewish literature and papyri, much of which has never been examined by previous scholars who worked on this subject.

My aim was not to find an easy answer but honestly to discover what the New Testament meant to its first hearers and readers. I made the wonderful discovery that the New Testament teaching is eminently practical and that it demonstrates God's continuing love for us, even after the sin of breaking marriage vows. I found that both Jesus and Paul condemned groundless divorce, but both allowed the victim of broken marriage vows to divorce. I also found that divorce implied the right to remarry.

Other scholars have come to the same conclusions simply by applying common sense – though they failed to find a Biblical basis for them. I was much more fortunate than them because of the unequalled access which I had to historical and cultural data about the context of the New Testament.

My parting plea to you is that you do not judge other scholars harshly for what they did not know, but please do apply critical judgement to what I have said. Do not simply accept what you have read here, or simply dismiss it, but consider the evidence and pray about it. I have tried to hear what God says to us all by listening in on what he said to 1st-century believers, but whether or not I have succeeded is for you to judge.

# Study Group Briefing Notes and Discussion Questions

These discussion sessions can be used in a Bible study setting or after a presentation based on the material in this book. Each session contains three parts:

- brief notes on a Bible passage which can be used as the basis of a study
- summary of relevant sections of this book which can be used as material for a presentation
- discussion questions.

The last of the six sessions is optional because it deals with the more general topic of how we read the Bible. This issue comes up in various sections of the book and is something which many people won't have thought through. You may decide that this topic is so fundamental that rather than leaving it to the end, the series should instead start with this session.

The questions are designed to provoke discussion rather than produce a straightforward answer, so the leader should use them as tools to produce an exchange of ideas. There is no need to answer them in the order presented or to complete all the questions.

A group will work well if the leader and the 'expert' are separate people. The 'expert' should give a talk or introduce the Bible passage and be familiar with the material. The leader should direct the discussion and keep everything moving. This does not mean that the leader should be the main speaker – he should in fact try to be the person who says the least because his main role is to encourage and aid the debate. The 'expert' should also try to keep out of the discussion except when the leader invites him to make a contribution.

In a group Bible study members will best remember the things they have found out for themselves and what they have said themselves. They may *possibly* remember what the 'expert' has said, and they will *probably* remember what other group members have said (especially if it was related to a story with emotional content). Therefore a successful group discussion is one where everyone feels that they have personally discovered something (so the 'expert' should leave some things to be 'discovered') and where everyone has contributed something to the discussion (so the leader should make sure everyone has their say).

## Study 1. Four grounds for divorce in the Old Testament

*Notes on Jeremiah 3.1–8*

**v. 1** Israel, the northern nation, had been divorced by God for her adultery, and she wanted to return. Jeremiah had doubts about this because Deuteronomy 24:1–4 says that a woman who has been divorced for her adultery and gone off to marry someone else cannot simply divorce her second husband and return to her first.

**vv. 2–3** God, through Jeremiah, reminded Israel that she had broken her marriage vows. She had taken lovers and although God tried to warn her to repent by withholding the rain, she refused to do so.
**vv. 4–5** Israel cried to God, calling him 'Father' and asking him to stop being angry with them. But they also continued in their sin so they clearly weren't genuinely repentant.

**v. 6** Jeremiah now turned to the southern nation of Judah and their new king, Josiah, who was one of the few good kings in the last years of this nation. Judah was falling into the same sin as Israel.

**vv. 7–8** Jeremiah tried to use the example of the northern nation of Israel to warn the nation of Judah. Even though Judah saw that God had divorced Israel, she still carried on committing the same spiritual adultery (v. 8).

## Summary of Chapter 2 re the ground of 'unfaithfulness' in Deuteronomy 24

The case which is recorded in Deuteronomy 24.1–4 concerns a woman who was divorced for "sexual immorality" (presumably adultery, though there are other possibilities), who then married someone else and finally wanted to remarry her first husband. This ruling said that she could not, though the reason isn't clear. Some scholars have suggested that it was to prevent the possibility of a husband 'pimping' his wife to a series of different 'husbands'.

This case provided the basis for the law that adultery was a ground for divorce, and thereby the basis for one of the marriage vows.

## Summary of Chapter 3 re three more grounds for divorce in Exodus 21

Exodus 21.10–11 is part of a law code, but the details are likely to be based on another actual case where a man took a slave as his wife and then later took a second wife. He was tempted to treat the second wife as his favourite but this ruling told him that he could not neglect his first wife by neglecting to give her food, clothing or physical affection. If this law applied to the least important member of society – a former slave – it is clearly a fundamental right for *every* married person.

This case provided the basis for the other three grounds for divorce and thereby the other three marriage vows.

## Discussion Questions

a. If you were asked to craft a law on divorce and decide the grounds on which one could get divorced, what grounds would you include? How would you word the corresponding marriage vows?

b. Moses gave all women in Israel a privilege that was only given to high-ranking women in other nations. Can you think of any extra privileges or opportunities which rich people have in our society when they are divorced? Does divorce make people better off or worse off?

c. Moses was particularly concerned for women because they suffered more than men when a marriage broke down. In what ways do men and women suffer differently in marriage break-up in our society, and who do you think suffers more? Who do you think are usually the ones who break their marriage vows – men or women?

d. Which OT picture of God's relationship with Israel works best for you – a peace treaty contract or a marriage contract? Which picture best illustrates your relationship with God? Are there other illustrations that you prefer?

e. How much do you think God's 'marriage' and 'divorce' was just an illustration? For example, which of the following do you think he actually experienced: love, disappointment, jealousy, anger, pain of separation, or loneliness after divorce? What other feelings can a divorced person experience?

f. The prophets do not appear to hesitate to talk about God as a divorcee. Why do you think this sounds so strange – and perhaps mildly blasphemous – to many Christians? Do you think 'divorcee' should be a negative label in today's so-ciety or in today's church?

## Study 2. Jesus' teaching on adultery and the new 'any cause' divorces

*Notes on Matthew 19.3–12*

**v. 3** The Question about Deuteronomy 24.1: The Pharisees asked Jesus what he thought about the new 'Any Cause' divorces.

**vv. 4–6** Jesus' digression: He didn't answer the Pharisees' question but talked about marriage, saying that it should be lifelong and monogamous.

**vv. 7–8** Back to the question: The Pharisees asked Jesus about the divorce certificate in Deuteronomy 24.1 – "isn't it compulsory sometimes (i.e. in cases of adultery)?" Jesus said, "No, but it is *permitted*, in cases of hard- heartedness."

**v. 9** Answering the question: Jesus says that Deuteronomy 24.1 does not allow divorce except for 'Sexual Immorality'. He also said that divorce for 'Any Cause' is invalid, so remarriage would be equivalent to adultery.

**vv. 10–12** Jesus taught that marriage isn't compulsory.

## Summary of Chapter 5 re Jesus' teaching

Deuteronomy 24.1 said that divorce is allowed for "a cause of sexual immorality". The Hillelites interpreted this to include both divorce for 'Any Cause' and for 'Sexual Immorality'. The Shammaites' interpretation was different, saying that there is no divorce (in Deut. 24.1) except for 'Sexual Immorality' and Jesus agreed with this.

## Summary of Chapter 8 (one section) 'Didn't Jesus allow only one ground for divorce?'

Jesus (and the Shammaites) did not mean that there were no grounds for divorce except for 'Sexual Immorality' *in the whole* OT, but this was the only ground in the phrase "a cause of sexual immorality" in Deut. 24.1.

## Discussion Questions

a. Why do you think that the 'Any Cause' divorce was so popular in Jesus' day? If people today had the choice of proving in court that their partner was adulterous, or of simply getting a quiet divorce, which would they choose? Do you think Joseph was wrong to choose this type of divorce?

b. Jesus said that you can divorce someone who 'hard-   heartedly' breaks their marriage vows, but how do you think this would work in practice? Who would decide that the person was 'hardhearted' (i.e. stubbornly unrepentant) – the other partner, their minister, or someone else? How long would you personally put up with a partner who did not provide material support or physical affection, or who was adulterous?

c. In a few Muslim countries, adultery is a criminal offence. Should Christians campaign for this in our country? If so, what do you think the penalty should be? Do you think divorce should be compulsory for adultery?

d. Jesus agreed with the Shammaites and quoted their slogan – do you think he was secretly a Shammaite? Do you think he should have avoided quoting their slogan and used his own words? Some

Christians have been labelled as Marxists in the past by using language like 'economic exploitation' – can you think of other examples where Christians get labelled by the language they use?

e.  How would you advise a couple or a family who were always having arguments about the best way to survive them?

## Study 3. Paul's teaching on the other three biblical grounds

*Notes on 1 Corinthians 7.1–15, 26–35*

**v. 1** The Corinthians had written to Paul asking what he thought about the saying, "It is good not to touch a woman."

**vv. 2–5** Paul said that married couples should not deprive each other because:
   a. they have made a vow, so they "owe" each other a "debt"
   b. prolonged abstinence leads to sexual temptation.

**vv. 6–9** Some people (like Paul) have the gift of singleness.

**vv. 10–11** If you are married, Paul said that you must not use the Roman divorce-by-separation by walking out or sending your partner out of your house. And if you have already done this, you should try to reverse it.

**vv. 12–14** If you have an unbelieving partner who is willing to stay, you should not initiate a divorce.

**vv. 15** If your unbelieving partner divorces you, there is nothing you can do but accept it.

**v. 26** The "present distress" (probably a famine) makes   marriage much more difficult at this time, so Paul advises people to wait if they can.
**vv. 27–28** Whatever state you are in, try to avoid getting married at present. You aren't sinning if you marry, but it won't be easy.

**vv. 29–31** These troubles may increase as they lead up to the end of the world!

**vv. 32–35** But if you are married, don't neglect your responsibilities to give material support to your partner and 'please' them with things of the world. If you aren't married, you can devote more time to serving the Lord.

### Summary of Chapter 6: Roman divorce-by-separation and modern groundless divorces

Paul approved of marriage in general, and emphasised the marriage vows that promised physical affection and material support (i.e. food and clothes).

Paul said that Christians should not use the Roman groundless divorce, and he assumed that no Christian would provide grounds for divorce by breaking their marriage vows. This means that only a non-Christian would cause a divorce.

If your non-Christian partner divorced you, there was no way under Roman law to prevent this so you should accept it.

### Summary of Chapter 8 (second half) re the four OT grounds for divorce in Paul

Paul regarded abandonment as a divorce based on the grounds of neglect. The vows to 'feed' and 'clothe' can be   generalised as material support. The vow to 'love' can be generalised as physical affection.

### Discussion Questions

a. Do you know any people who have felt that they were not allowed to divorce when common sense says that they should? Would this understanding of the Biblical grounds have helped them?

b. In what ways was the Roman world like the modern western world and in what ways was it different?

c. The Romans thought that it was immoral for people to have more than one wife, but that it was OK to divorce one day and get remarried the next. Which do you think is more immoral? Who are more immoral – a couple who live together faithfully without marrying, or someone who divorces and remarries four times consecutively?

d. When people wanted to divorce someone because they were a non-Christian, Paul said they should not (1 Cor. 7.12–13). But Paul also said that they shouldn't marry a non-Christian when they had the choice (1 Cor. 7.39). Do you think that he was being inconsistent? Do you think it is a sin for a Christian to marry a non-Christian or is it just unwise?

e. Paul advised the Corinthians not to get remarried during a famine because it would be hard to take care of the children. Do you think a famine would be a reason to avoid marriage in our society? In what kind of circumstances would you advise someone not to get married? In what circumstances would you advise someone to *get* married?

f. Some Christians in Corinth thought that a celibate lifestyle was superior to a married one. Do you think that this might be true for some people? How would someone know if this was the right path for themselves? Do you think that it is still correct, like in Paul's day, that a single person has more time for serving the Lord?

g. Rabbinic Jews before the time of Jesus needed to decide when someone had broken their marriage vows, so they defined how much money the man had to spend on food and clothes, and how much cooking and sewing the woman had to do. They even defined how often the man had to perform his conjugal duties! How could we tell when someone has broken their marriage vows without making similar definitions? When would you say that someone was guilty of neglecting material needs? When would you say that someone was guilty of neglecting physical affection?

## Study 4. 'Till death us do part' and remarriage

*Notes on 1 Corinthians 7.10–15, 39–40*

**vv. 10–11** Paul told those who were married not to use the Roman divorce-by-separation, and if they had done so already, then they must remain unmarried so that they can be reconciled if possible.

**vv. 12–14** If you are married to an unbeliever it is still a holy marriage and you must not break it up.

**v. 15** If the unbeliever walks out, there is nothing you can do to save the marriage because this is legal divorce, and there is nothing you can do to bring about reconciliation because they have chosen to end it. Therefore you are 'no longer bound' – i.e. you are free to remarry.

**vv. 39–40** Widows are also free to remarry, and (contrary to the Levirate law of Deut. 25.5-10) Christian widows can marry whoever they want, so long as they marry a Christian.

### Summary of Chapter 7 re texts which appear to deny remarriage before a partner dies.

Matthew. 19.5 '…one flesh' is not an irreversible oneness, otherwise anyone who visited a prostitute before conversion could not marry (cf. 1 Cor. 6.15–20).

Matthew. 19.6 ' …*let* no-one separate' implies that one can separate, but should not unless there are Biblical grounds.

Matthew. 19.9 seems to imply that a divorcee is still married in God's eyes, but the context is about those who have an invalid divorce based on 'Any Cause' and not about divorces on Biblical grounds.

Romans 7.2 does not mention divorce because this is not a teaching about marriage and divorce but a picture of marriage to the Law and then to Christ. The Law is like a very upright and correct man who would never break any marriage vows so there would never be grounds for a divorce.

1 Corinthians 7.39–40 does not mention divorce because it is addressing widows.

### Summary of Chapter 9: Everyone, including Paul, assumed that divorcees could remarry

Everyone in Jewish society assumed remarriage was a right, and it was a duty if they did not have children. Everyone in Roman society regarded remarriage as a legal obligation.

Paul quietly assumes that Christians can remarry. If he wanted to say that they could not he would have needed to say so very clearly indeed.

### Summary of Chapter 10: Should you get divorced if you remarry after an invalid divorce?

Re-divorce is breaking a new set of marriage vows and two wrongs don't make a right.

Matthew 5 puts Jesus' saying about 'remarriage is adultery' with other examples of preacher's rhetoric like 'anger is the same as murder' and 'cut off the offending organ'. Even in this section, Jesus did not tell anyone to divorce their new partner.

### Discussion Questions

a. Paul said Judaism was like being married to the Law and Christianity was like being married to Christ (Rom. 7.1–4). What does this imply about differences between Christianity and Judaism? Do you think that these two faiths are still different in these same ways? If not, which has changed?

b. When Romans became decadent and luxury-loving, they had far fewer children, so Augustus passed laws to encourage marriage and child-bearing. Most developed countries are now in a similar situation. Do you think it is time that Christians taught 'go forth and multiply' as a command from God?

c. If people are having trouble with their marriage, God wants to help heal the breakdown. What kind of things should we be praying for, to help them? Is there anything else that we can do without intruding into their privacy?

d. Jesus said polygamy was not what God intended, even in the Old Testament. Does this mean that Abraham, Jacob, David etc. were sinning by having extra wives? What do you think missionaries should say to converts who have more than one wife – should they tell them to divorce all but one wife? If so, who should look after the divorced wives, and should they be allowed to remarry?

e. Paul told the person who divorced without good grounds to remain unmarried and try to become reconciled. Do you think that they are free from this command if the other person rejects their offer of reconciliation and marries someone else? When can you be sure that the other person won't change their mind?

## Study 5. Wedding vows, and remarriage in church

### Notes on Ephesians 5.21–33

**v. 21** This ends the previous section with 'submit to each other', then v. 22 onwards looks at the details about who submits to whom, and how.

**vv. 22–24** Wives submit like we all submit to Christ.
**vv. 25–27** Husbands love sacrificially, like Christ.
**vv. 28–29** Keep the marriage vows (to love, feed and clothe) like Christ does.
**vv. 30–33** Husbands and wives become one, like we become one with Christ.

## Summary of Chapter 11 re modern marriage vows

Our marriage vows come from Exodus 21.10 via Ephesians 5.28–29 and have not changed much except that the language is a bit more formal.

The vow to 'obey' is new – this was added in Roman times in an attempt to bring order back into society using Aristotle's philosophy. Early Christians were not entirely happy with it and taught a modified version of this morality.

When broken vows result in divorce, we should certainly allow the innocent partner to remarry in church, but what about the guilty one? Perhaps after a service of Repentance for Broken Promises?

## Summary of Chapter 14 (second half) re church practice

Similar conclusions to those in this book have been found by previous scholars though the new evidence now makes them difficult to ignore

These conclusions are useful in marriage counselling but many churches are too reliant on tradition for their practices to change at this stage.

## Discussion Questions

a. What do you think the church should do to encourage people to get married and to discourage divorce? Should we discourage church attendance by unmarried couples or bar them from membership? If people are put off by expensive weddings, is there anything we can do about it?

b. What do you think the government should do to encourage people to get married and to discourage divorce? Should the tax system benefit married couples? Should children born to married partners be given special recognition? Should schools teach against living together without marriage?

c. In marriage vows, we promised to feed, clothe and love each other, in faithfulness. If you have taken marriage vows, were you aware of what they contained? Did you have any pre-marriage counselling on these vows? Do you think the vows should be different now?

d. If you are married, can you remember if you vowed to 'obey'? If you were to marry tomorrow would you want to promise this to your husband or wife? What does this vow mean to you?

e. Broken vows can lead to broken marriages. Do you think that we should let the person who broke their vows remarry in church? In what way might a service of Repentance for Broken Promises be helpful? Would you let someone marry the lover with whom they committed adultery, in church?

f. Do you think that the church should change its teaching when later research reveals more about what the Bible means? Do discoveries like these make you feel uneasy or excited? Do you think the scholars were influenced by changes in modern society? Should the church depend more on tradition and less on the Bible in order to avoid such changes?

## Study 6 (optional). How to read the Bible, including the Old Testament

*Notes on Matthew 5.17-48*

**vv. 17–20,48** Jesus demands a *higher* regard for the OT than the Pharisees. The following examples show that he applied OT principles very widely but did not always apply the details of the OT.

**vv. 21–26** The OT says murder is wrong which implies the principle that whatever leads to murder (such as hatred) is also wrong.

**vv. 27–32** The OT says adultery is wrong, which implies the principle that anything which leads to adultery is also wrong – such as illicit lust or invalid divorces.

**vv. 33–37** The OT says it is wrong to lie to God, which implies the principle that it is wrong to lie to anyone.

**vv. 38–42** The OT limits revenge to the degree of your loss, which implies the principle that we should limit or even forego revenge.

**vv. 43–47** The OT says love your neighbour which implies the principle that we should love everyone, including our enemies.

### Summary of Chapter 4 re the Old Testament for New Testament believers

Which parts of the Old Testament apply to Christians?
a. only the moral laws and not the ceremonial laws?
b. only the principles and not the details?
c. only the laws affirmed in the New Testament?

Many modern legal systems are based on the Old Testament, especially in Exodus 21 where law about divorce for neglect occurs.

### Summary of Chapter 7: section re 'the argument from silence'

Silence is very significant when it is surprising, like when Jesus listed to the Rich Young Ruler all of the 10 Commandments which concern people (i.e. Num. 5–10) and omitted the last one – the one about coveting (Mt. 19.16–22).

Silence is not significant when it is not surprising, such as when we do not hear that Adam woke from his sleep after Eve was made.

Silence is certainly not significant when the *mention* of something would be surprising, such as the two passages where death is mentioned as a way to end a marriage, but not divorce. The first (Rom. 7.2) concerns Jewish believers who are married to the law, and the second (1 Cor. 7.39) concerns widows, so in both cases it would be inappropriate to talk about these people being divorced.

### Summary of Chapter 10 (one section) re Preachers' Rhetoric

Jesus was using preachers' rhetoric when he told people to gouge out the eyes which led them to commit adultery in their hearts.

### Summary of Chapter 12 (2nd half): 20th century readers have to work hard

The Bible comes to us in a foreign language and from a foreign culture, so we have to learn about both of these in order to know what

God told the first readers – because only then can we understand what he says to us. We have books and experts to help us, so we know much more about the 1st-century than even a 2nd-century believer.

The Reformation principle of *Sola Scriptura* says that what we need to know for salvation is plainly understood from Scripture, though the Reformers said that many other things were "not plain in themselves, nor clear unto… the unlearned".

## Discussion Questions

a. Many Old Testament laws no longer apply to Christians in the New Testament, such as the Festivals, sacrifices, or the death penalty for adultery or blasphemy. How do you think we should decide if a law still applies to us today? Does this mean we have the right to pick and choose which of God's laws we should keep?

b. Many of our modern laws are based on Old Testament principles. Are there others which you think we should follow today? E.g.:

   – give a second tithe for the poor every three years (Deut. 14.28–29)

   – do not destroy the environment during war (Deut. 20.19).

c. Many church leaders in the 18th and 19th centuries criticised the introduction of musical instruments into worship, and some still do. Do you think the fact that instruments are not mentioned in NT worship is significant in this debate? If the New Testament doesn't say whether we should use instruments or not, how should we know what is right?

d. Jesus did not mean us literally to cut off organs which lead us to illicit lust, but some, like Origen in the 2nd century, interpreted it literally – though he interpreted it non-literally in his commentary on Matthew which he wrote several years after castrating himself. How can we tell when Jesus is being literal and when he is using preacher's rhetoric? Should we literally turn the other cheek (Mt. 5.39) and refuse to take oaths in court (Mt. 5.34–37)?

e. The church has split many times in history over doctrinal matters – the Trinity, date of Easter, authority of the Pope, role of priests, tongues, status of women, eschatology etc. Why do you think the

Holy Spirit lets us get confused about these things? Why do you think that Scripture was not written more straightforwardly? Do you think there would be fewer splits or more splits if women were in charge?

f. How do you personally decide what a difficult scripture means? E.g.:

> – 'on this rock I will build my church' (Mt. 16.18): some people (mainly Catholics) think the rock is Peter while others (mainly Protestants) think it is the statement which Jesus has just made.

> – 'when perfection comes' (1 Cor. 13.10): some people (mainly Charismatics) think this is the coming of Christ while others (mainly those who think the Gifts ended in the 1st century) think that this is the completion of the New Testament.

# Notes

1 The code of Hammurabi contains laws which established order in society, for example:

> #233: If a builder constructs a house and does faulty work resulting in an unsafe wall, then the builder must pay to strengthen that wall at his own expense.
> But when accidents are out of someone's control they were not considered to be a crime, such as:
> #244: If a citizen rents an ox or an ass and if a lion kills it while it is out in the open then there is no fine.

This set of laws even gives us the first instance of an 'act of God' which modern insurance salesmen often have difficulty defining:

> #249: If a citizen rents an ox and a member of the divine assembly strikes it with lightning and it dies, then the citizen who had rented the ox must swear in the name of a member of the divine assembly that the death of the ox was an act of God, and then there is no fine.

2 Hammurabi Code #36: If her husband has gone off to the fields, …If she has gone to live with a(nother) husband before the five years and has also borne children, her husband upon coming back shall get her back and her children as well because she did not respect the marriage covenant but got married.
3 Hammurabi Code #196–199: If a citizen blinds the eye of an official, then his eye is to be blinded. If a citizen blinds the eye… of someone who is not a citizen, the fine is 18 ounces of silver. If one citizen blinds the eye… of another citizen's slave, then the fine is half the price of the slave.
4 For example, Middle Assyrian Code #A9: If one citizen forces the wife of another to let him kiss her, then his lower lip is drawn along the edge of an axe blade and cut off.

5 Middle Assyrian law #A45: When a woman has been given in marriage and the enemy has captured her husband, ...she shall complete two years and then she may go to live with the husband of her choice. They shall write a tablet for her as a widow.

The right of a widow is given in Middle Assyrian Law #A33: "she may go where she wishes". This occurs frequently in ANE legal documents and means "she may go to live with whoever she wishes".

6 The phrase is *'ervat debar'*, where the first word means 'nakedness' or 'sexual immorality' and the second word is a 'thing' or a multitude of other meanings including 'cause' or 'reason' as in 1 Kings 9.15 or Joseph 5.4. The phrase only occurs elsewhere in Deuteronomy 23.14 with regard to modesty in the camp's toilet arrangements. The translation "a matter of sexual immorality" or "a cause of sexual immorality" fits well in the context and according to ancient Jewish interpretations it means the woman was guilty of adultery.

7 This follows the ESV except that 'conjugal love' replaces 'marital rights' which is confusing here because 'food' and 'clothing' can also said to be 'marital rights'.

8 The ESV and other recent translations speak about "the man who hates and divorces" so that God is not the one who "hates" anything. This is undoubtedly a better translation, but it is still true that this passage shows God's extreme dislike of divorce.

9 As noted before, the ESV actually reads "some indecency", which is translated here as "a cause of sexual immorality" because it is somewhat more literal and it fits with the terminology used throughout this book.

10 In my academic work I have translated this as the 'Any Matter' divorce because this helps to convey the overlap between the Hebrew *debar* and the Greek *aitian*. The translation 'Any Cause' leans more towards the *Greek* than the Hebrew.

11 This is found in *Sifré* Deuteronomy 269; Jerusalem Talmud *Sotah* 1.2, 16b and Mishnah *Gittin* 9.10. The Greek of Matthew 19.9 ('whoever divorces his wife except for sexual immorality') is almost exactly the same, because both Jesus and Shammai use the typically Jewish expression 'not if' to mean 'except', and both use a vague general word for 'sexual immorality' rather than a specific word meaning 'adultery'. The version in Mishnah *Gittin* 9.10 is different only by one word because it says "except he has found 'a matter of sexual immorality'" which is exactly like the different version of Jesus' saying in Matthew 5.32: "Every one who divorces his wife, except for 'a matter of sexual immorality'". The word 'matter' in Matthew 5.32 (Greek *logos*) has the same range of meaning as 'matter' in Shammai's saying which quotes Deuteronomy 24.1 (Hebrew *debar*, 'a word' or 'a thing'). I cannot think of any way in which

Shammai's phrase could be translated more accurately into Greek than in these words of Jesus.

12 Philo used it in *Special Laws* 3.30: "Another commandment is that if a woman after parting from her husband for 'Any Cause'…". Josephus used it in *Antiquities of the Jews* 4.253: "He who desires to be divorced from the wife who is living with him for 'Any Cause' (and with mortals many such may arise), must certify in writing …". In the Rabbinic commentary *Sifré Deuteronomy* 269 the Hillelites say that a man can divorce a woman even if she spoiled his dinner, since it says '[Any] Cause', and then they go on to defend their conclusion that Deuteronomy 24.1 speaks both about "she who is divorced for 'A Cause'" and "she who is divorced for 'Sexual Immorality'".

13 The ESV translates 'dismiss' as 'divorce', which is accurate but it might suggest that 'separate' does not also imply 'divorce'.

14 A more literal translation of 'separates' is possible, but it would be much more clumsy. As discussed previously in this chapter, the verb 'separate' is reflexive, so it should be translated "separate himself", but the Greek could mean male or female (as the context confirms when Paul calls their partner "brother or sister") so that a literal translation would be: "If the unbeliever separates themselves, let them separate themselves ." The translation 'not enslaved' in the ESV is a very good literal translation, though most versions have something less strong like 'not bound'. We will see in chapter 9 that 'not enslaved' is appropriate because it is referring back to the context of Exodus 21.10 which concerns slavery.

15 As before, the ESV 'divorce' has been translated more literally as 'dismiss'.

16 Some of the early Church Fathers actually thought that this silence was significant. Clement of Alexandria in the 2nd century said that "Jesus ate and drank in a special manner without giving forth the food again" (*Miscellanies* 3.7.59).

17 Origen *Matthew* II.14.24.

18 As we saw in chapter 5, all these subjects are dealt with in Matthew 19.3–12 and some of them in Mark 10.2–12.

19 Literally "for a man to divorce his wife".

20 See Jerusalem Talmud *Sotah* 1.2, 16b. This misunderstanding is expressed by R. Yose b. Zabida and his son R. Eleazar soon after AD 300.

21 As before, 'marital rights' in the ESV has been changed to a more literal 'conjugal rights' because food and clothing can equally be called 'marital rights' in this context.

22 Examples are listed in Mishnah *Ketubah* 7.2–5.

23 A copy of the *Damascus Document* was actually discovered 50 years before the Dead Sea Scrolls in the late 1890s as part of the 'Geniza' collection which is described in chapter 11.

24 The NIV is quoted here – the ESV has a slightly more accurate but more archaic way of putting this: "Slaves are to be submissive to their own masters in everything… so that in everything they may adorn the doctrine of God our Saviour."

25 We saw in chapter 8 that even some rabbis misunderstood the Shammaite slogan just a couple of centuries later.

26 This is a literal translation. Modern versions often try to retain the anatomical references by misleadingly translating it "heart and mind".

27 Tertullian, *Wife* I.7. This was written before he joined the ascetic sect of Montanists, so this was his viewpoint while he was still a church leader in mainstream Christianity.

28 Alford said: "This was a question of dispute between the rival Rabbinical schools of Hillel and Shammai; the former asserting the right of arbitrary divorce, from Deuteronomy 24.1, the other denying it except in cases of adultery." He also quoted the use of the phrase 'Any Cause' in Josephus *Antiquities*. 4.253.

29 The Greek *monandros* or its Latin equivalent *univera* is common on funeral inscriptions in praise of someone who was faithful to her husband. See references in Craig Keener, *…And Marries Another* (Hendrickson, 1991) 92–93.